MW01643911

Cinzano. Champion, Convict and Legend.

1st digital edition (Spanish), March 2022.

1st print edition (Spanish), April 2022.

2nd print edition (Spanish), September 2022.

ISBN: 978-9915-41-022-7204

1st digital edition, USA edition, December 2024

1st Amazon print edition, USA edition, December 2024

ISBN: 9798304424271

Author: Daniel Torres Rodríguez

Contact: cinzanolibro@gmail.com

Instagram: @cinzanoCCL

Cover design:

Martín Ocretich: boxingbear@gmail.com

Copyediting (Spanish version):

María Fernanda Rey: mafernanda_rey@hotmail.com

Translation:

Carolina Gazzaneo and Paola Gazzaneo

Wise Language Solutions - http://wise-ls.com

212 Pages. 152,4 x 215,9 mm.

Independently published

"Cinzano — Champion, Convict and Legend" is one of the best books of the year."

Federico Medina, La Diaria, July of 2022.

"Daniel Torres has the virtue of narrating the plot in three chapters in a colloquial, engaging, seasoned, and entertaining manner."

Leonardo Ferber, Eleturf, May of 2022.

"The story seems as if taken from a screenplay."

Andrés López Reilly, El País, May of 2022.

CINZANO

CHAMPION, CONVICT and LEGEND

ACKNOWLEDGMENTS

This book would never have seen the light of day without the collaboration of Luis Costa Baleta, Leonardo Ferber, Gustavo Iribarren, Pablo Innella, Jerome Vonk, Martín Ocretich, Héctor Díaz, Marcelo Silveira, Yhonny Hernández, Walter Báez, Álvaro Mattos, Michele O'Brien, Randy Rouse, William McCormick, and my family.

This English translation would not have been possible without Michele O'Brien's immense generosity; there are simply not enough words to express my gratitude to her.

PREFACE

While I was writing this book, I received two pieces of advice. The first, as soon as the idea came to be, was from around 2011: “It’s a great story, but you’d better write it quickly, because this happened over thirty years ago, and time waits for no one.” I didn’t pay attention, and, after many failed beginnings and nearly endless desertions, by the end of 2021, I had completed it. Ten years is not particularly fast, and time passed for many of the characters. Our conversations with Randy Rouse turned out to be all too few before his death in 2016.

Panchito Costa Baleta was the one to give me the final push: in July 2021, he called to tell me he needed an article for the Museum of Horse Racing about Cinzano’s tour in the U.S., nothing too long because people don’t read anymore —especially on the Internet. That was how, writing those three or four pages, I got reacquainted with information I had gathered before, discovered “new” information, and got once again sucked into the "Cinzano-Lebón" universe. This time, for good.

Conversations with Panchito became more frequent, as did the exchange of documentation. But by the time I was finishing the first draft, the news of his death came as a big blow. One of the driving forces behind this book was not going to be able to see it in print—the advice from ten years ago slapped me hard in the face again. Since that day, and until the moment this arrived at the printer's, there were no more pauses or excuses; "better late than never" is a phrase I hate, but I accepted it with a dose of resignation.

The other piece of advice I got during the book's first proofreading was: "You have to mention it was Uranio's grandson and part of the lineage of Congreve. Not acknowledging Congreve is not an option: *"...y hoy, que tengo la cabeza / cubierta con tanta nieve, / con los hijos de Congreve / vuelvo a rejuvenecer"* [...and today, with my head / covered in so much snow, / with Congreve's sons / I am young again"]. It appears in *Milonga que peina canas*[1], it has to be in the book." I regret to admit I did not follow this advice either; this is the second to last mention of Congreve, despite being well aware of its record as a champion producer in Argentina and its overall contribution to breeding in the Rio de la Plata.

Between unheeded advice and nights scouring

[1] Translator's Note: *Milonga que peina canas* is a 1942 *milonga* by Alberto Gómez, that mentions several Argentine racehorses.

newspapers.com, this book took shape during the last few months of 2021. The seed had been planted in 2011, but its story had already captivated me four years prior, when I inadvertently stumbled into the news that a horse called Cinzano had been inducted into the Hall of Fame of the Virginia Steeplechase Association (VSA.) Could it be the Uruguayan horse? The ease of the Internet, coupled with some idle time at work, confirmed this suspicion and led me to the story of the horse as told by the North American media. I was more or less acquainted with the local legend: the mafia, a veterinarian who worked for them, Telly Savalas, and the murder of Lebón. When I realized that everything I had learned was a lie and that the story was entirely different, I became a sort of Xeroque Rolmes—the name given by Brazilians to pseudo-sleuths—, Googling like crazy and diving into free magazine libraries. I assembled an archive that, at least for now, would allow me to tell the story at the tables of Santa Catalina,[2] when we embarked on late-night horseracing journeys.

The more I discovered and wrote, the less I understood why no one had yet turned this story into a movie. If someone were to write fiction with this plot, it would be dismissed as too wild. From the moment the horses arrived in the United States, everything that transpired seems unlikely—fortunately, it is recorded in the papers of the time, dispelling any doubts about its occurrence. As of now, this record will also be available,

[2] Translator's Note: Santa Catalina is a bar in downtown Montevideo.

seeking to vindicate one of the best horses our country has produced in the last forty-five years, and shed light on the legend surrounding the affair. This way, whenever someone mentions Cinzano in the future, we can discuss with a bit more certainty—and perhaps even embellish the stories further—but always grounded in actual facts.

PREFACE TO THE ENGLISH VERSION

It is strange to write something knowing it will be translated into another language. Let alone give it the title of "preface", knowing well in advance that this is not what it is, but rather some clarifications I deem worthy to make, since the original version was written in the Spanish variant of the Rio de la Plata and intended for Uruguayan and Argentinian audiences. I am not implying it cannot be read in other Spanish-speaking regions, but I am sure someone from the Rio de la Plata might have a better grasp of the nuances, and I know that our dear English readers will find many things strange, even unintelligible. Please know that before sending the manuscript to the translator, I made my best effort to transform certain regional slang into something more "universal." Whether I succeeded or not, I'll never know, because my English is on par with Tarzan's. In any case, I always have an ace up my sleeve: blame it on the translation.

I cannot conclude this initial diatribe without mentioning Michele O'Brien, the person to whom we entirely owe the fact that you are reading this in English. Without her, I would never be able to boast to my writer friends that I published a book in two languages. I owe Michele eternal gratitude, and I send her the biggest possible hug one can give through a piece of paper.

CHAMPION

Without anyone knowing, Cinzano's film would begin rolling with a sharp strike of the gavel and the auctioneer's shout at the Haras Yaguarí: "Sold!" Roberto Forné, a successful Uruguayan entrepreneur, owner of the Valor stud, and buyer of the colt—the son of Tudor Park and Lee—was in charge of the executive production. The movie featured Hollywood's classical narrative: a dreamy beginning, the subsequent fall from grace, and, finally, redemption, accompanied by never-ending joy.

But every film starts somewhere, and that story is rarely one to transcend. This one, in particular, was forged between a trip to Venezuela and an unsuccessful mare in the Maroñas horsetrack.

Months before the auction, Walter Báez[1] had had his eye set on Doña Tola (offspring of Weedon Hill and Brasilia), a winning mare in a couple of short-distance races. The mare was put up for sale on a Sunday in Maroñas, and the young Báez

---

1 A living legend of Uruguayan horse racing. With more than sixty years in horse racing, he holds the national record for races won both as jockey (1,651 victories) and as trainer (1,360 wins). No matter how much his career is praised, it is not enough.

offered 900 pesos, which were enough for him to secure the specimen. A different challenge awaited him now: having Pablo Gelsi[2] accept training the broodmare, since the experienced caretaker thought being the owner wasn't compatible with being the jockey. Finally, Gelsi caved into his son-in-law's arguments (yes, they were also related) and got to work. After a while, Doña Tola reappeared in a 1500-meter stakes, a distance seemingly impossible given her history. However, guided by Báez's masterful hand, she showcased her progress and claimed victory. Unfortunately, after crossing the finish line, the mare suffered a severe injury, and they immediately decided to end her racing career. With his hopes shattered, Báez took the future broodmare to Haras Yaguarí and, in return, received a voucher for 4000 pesos to use at any of their auctions. Thus ended his jockey-slash-owner adventure—for now.

When Haras Yaguarí published the catalog for the auction of horses born in 1973, Walter Báez was about to depart for Venezuela, where he would represent Uruguay in an international jockey competition. With that catalog as his travel reading, he arrived in the Caribbean country and, upon reaching the La Rinconada racetrack, saw a huge mural of the Uruguayan horse Carpintero, a multiple stakes winner in Venezuela and

---

2 One of the best trainers in the history of Uruguayan horse racing. Winner of 930 races, he was a specialist in preparing horses for long distances: he won four *Gran Premio Ramírez*, seven *Gran Premio Nacional*, and eight *Gran Premio General Artigas*, among other stakes. He marked an era and a style at the old Maroñas.

record-holder at 3200 meters. He immediately remembered that this horse was the offspring of Imaginado and Annabel Lee, so he looked at the catalog again to confirm what he had read. One of the horses being auctioned was also a son of Annabel Lee: Cinzano.

Convinced it was rather a revelation than a hunch, when he came back to Uruguay, he walked up to his father in law to propose the business deal: buying Cinzano between the two, using Doña Tola's voucher. After some back-and-forth, Gelsi agreed, and they both went to the auction, with the hopes of bringing home the son of Annabel Lee, which they did for a sum of 8500 pesos. The following day, Báez ran into Roberto Forné, whom he knew from before. He told him about his purchase at the Haras Yaguarí. The businessman got excited and asked the jockey if he could take part in the deal: "I'll talk to Don Pablo and let you know", was the response. During that conversation, his father-in-law put his years of experience ahead of passion and said: "you married my daughter recently, those 4000 pesos will come in handy now. I will take care of the horse, and you will race it; if it's any good, we'll win just as well. I'll head to the office now to complete the payment, but tell Forné he can have it for the same amount we paid." To Gelsi's surprise, someone had already taken care of that: Forné had stopped by the office minutes before to secure his participation in the colt. This is how, forty-eight hours after being purchased by Walter Báez, the horse was transferred to the partnership led by Roberto Forné, and everything was in place for the start of this movie in real time.

Days later, Báez began training the colt and quickly found out the animal was special—it was very smart, an essential trait in every champion. There's a saying that goes: "Not all smart horses are champions, but all champions are smart horses," which, in this case, fit perfectly. When Cinzano was taken to the boxes owned by Pablo Gersi in Maroñas, he not only showed intelligence but also exhibited athletic qualities rarely seen. The horse responded even better as the tasks got more demanding, and Gelsi was indeed a demanding trainer. From the moment they arrived at the training grounds, he also molded his running style, aiming to control his impulse in the first half of the race to unleash his speed in the final stretch, where races are often decided. His progress was steady, and in the mornings, he was one of the most talked-about colts. And I say mornings because in the afternoons, the most famous one was Capitel (Alignment and Capital), a chestnut trained by Fredy Trías[3] and also ridden by Walter Báez. Undefeated in two races, even a stakes against Mogambo (Ujier and Yaguasa, a descendent of the great Yatasto) on June 13, he entered the triple crown selection process with the honor of being the leader among the colts.

---

3 Fredy Trías, Uruguayan trainer active between 1950 until February 18, 2001, when he died at the same time as his horse, Hobbes, won a race at the Las Piedras racetrack. Among his most notable horses is Kumis, the historic mare from the Caraguatá stud, who won the *Gran Premio*

The debut of Cinzano came late, just one month before the *Polla de Potrillos*, on July 4, 1976, in the three-year-old maiden category over a distance of 1500 meters. Eight rivals were originally registered, but only four showed up: Scrouchante, Galache, Evasivo, and Abd-El-Krim, who, in that order and by several lengths, followed the son of Tudor Park, who stopped the clocks at 1 min 31 s 3/5, a normal time for the category, but which gains value when we read the race reports:

> Cinzano earned his reputation
>
> Cinzano has fully justified everything good that has been said about him for quite some time now. ¡Damn! Báez did no more than 'hold him back' throughout the entire duration of the meet, and he prevailed by a length, virtually 'flowering' in 1'31" 3/5 for the 1500 meters.
>
> [...]
>
> The truth is that, after this display, it is not hard to imagine that this Cinzano character could be among the 'colts of the year'.

The race could well have been a 'show of force for money,' as is common parlance, since he started well and Báez held him back. During the first 300 meters of the race, he had positioned himself third without any effort, moved into second midway through the turn, and entering the final stretch, took the lead and increased his advantage without his jockey asking for

Municipal, among other stakes.

the slightest effort. The theory of the 'show of force for money' gains strength because, one week later, he once again raced the same distance as in his debut, but in a stake, and against company that, in advance, seemed to be more challenging.

Six rivals came out to challenge him in the Guzmán Vargas Stakes disputed on July 11, in the order in which they came in: Engranaje, Marineto, Cacho M, Arlequino, Don Eloy and Zoco. Once again, he won by several lengths, but in this case, his time showed the horse meant business: 1 min 29 s 3/5. The strategy was the same as in his debut, he maintained his position at the back, waiting, ultimately gaining positions at the turn, taking the lead at the start of the final straight, and extending his advantage to the finish line without ever being pushed to his limits. The press had no doubts about Cinzano's running ability, but hinted that we would see his true potential when another horse of similar caliber put him under pressure.

As often happens with colts that have yet to face the best of their generation, neither the press nor the audience risk putting them on a pedestal, no matter how spectacular their triumphs. In horse racing, we are always waiting for a champion, but that doesn't mean we hand out praise to just anyone; by no means, they have to earn it on the track, running up against the very best. The matter is that Cinzano appeared to come into the *Polla de Potrillos*, to be disputed on August 8, 1976, undefeated, and his trainer, Pablo Gelsi, interviewed by *El País*, had unwavering confidence in the virtues of his protégé:

> Cinzano runs faster with each passing day. From one week to the next, he improved by two seconds, which is insane… This son of Tudor Park must be something else. He is just like Mi Tocayo, and they might even resemble each other in their running style due to their lineage, the former, son of Uranio, and Cinzano, grandson of Congreve's memorable son. The advantage I have with Cinzano is that we trained him as a colt to run from the back, to make the most of his great speed in the final stretch.
>
> […]
>
> If the *Polla* were next Sunday, I would tell you it wouldn't be easy to beat him. I say this because in horse racing there are no certainties.

Given the circumstances, the *Polla de Potrillos* promised to be an exciting one, with four top contenders: Cinzano, Capitel, Mogambo and Dioríssimo (Heathen and Dione). If it wasn't the best generation of the last forty-five years, it sure came close, because there have been many champions in the history of Maroñas, but I don't remember that many on a single generation. Getting into that game that we horse racing enthusiasts enjoy so much, the generation born in 1987 comes to mind, with Adyacente (Group 1 in Argentina), Mercenario (Group 3 in Argentina and winner of the *Gran Premio José Pedro Ramírez*) and Don Omar (winner of the *Polla de Potrillos* and *Gran Premio Piñeyrúa*, an excellent maternal grandsire) or, closer in time, the generation of Invasor (Best horse in the world 2007) and Potri Flash (Group 1 in Argentina.)

Obviously, Walter Báez would cease to ride Capitel and stay with Cinzano, while Pedro Hernández would ride the son of Alignment. Mogambo would continue with Jorge Firpo, and Dioríssimo would be ridden by the Chilean jockey Sergio Vera, who was replacing Carlos Gómez. Outsider Rich Speech (Current Speech and Bather) was added to the 'Four Aces'—he was a chestnut from the Haras La Quebrada stud, who was crossing the river with intentions of taking the prize. He would be ridden by the Venezuelan jockey Justo Torres and had noteworthy credentials at the Hipódromo Argentino de Palermo.

The *Polla de Potrillos* is in existence since 1907. The first gem in the Uruguayan Triple Crown, it is run over 1600 meters. The *Polla de Potrancas* is its counterpart for fillies and the only leg in the Triple Crown that is run separately. The Triple Crown is a series of three races over 60 days, reserved for colts and fillies aged three years old. The two races that follow the *Pollas* are the *Gran Premio Jockey Club* over 2000 meters, and the *Gran Premio Nacional* over 2500 meters. Both can be contested by both colts and fillies. If it is extremely difficult for a colt to win the Triple Crown, it is even more so for a fillie—the only case in the history of Maroñas occurred in 1915 with Verona, a daughter of Maroñas and Folie, ridden by Medardo Bonilla, trained by Eduvijes Melo, representing the stud Imperio, and bred at Haras Hampton. The total number of Triple Crown winners since 1907 (the first time it was contested) to date, counting the aforementioned Verona, is twenty-two. The last was Sir Fever in 2014, the first was

Ricaurte in 1913, and the best of them all, without a doubt, was Invasor (sorry about that, Romántico), who conquered the feat in 2006. When buying a colt or filly, an owner can only hope to take part in one of the stakes, because it puts them in the running for the Triple Crown. For the international reader, the equivalent of the *Polla de Potrillos* or *Potrancas* would be the 2000 and 1000 Guineas, respectively, or the *Poule d'Essai des Poulaines* and *des Pouliches* in France. Among the notable winners I recall who were not Triple Crown winners, I could mention Leicester, a son of Legendario who was close to winning the Triple Crown, the undefeated Quiqueño—my favorite horse growing up and with whom Walter Báez was about to win the Triple Crown in his double role as jockey and trainer—, Centaurus—an Argentine from the stud La Felicidad who once won a stakes by fifty-two lengths—, Ocean Pearl—who won it with Rubén Indaburu, a jockey from Colonia, at over 100 pesos per ticket—, Mount Royal—who later won the Joaquín Anchorena (Group 1) at San Isidro—, Bien Guapo—who wasn't among the best, but was from Colonia and my chauvinism just kicked in. From our modern era, I remember the victories of Davide, a running machine, like Boby di Job, another spectacular winner and Ajuste Fiscal, who proudly flew the Uruguayan flag high at the 2021 Dubai meeting.

In 1976, sixteen colts were entered in the *Polla de Potrillos*, but on Sunday at the starting post, only ten showed up. Amateur, Estirado, Label, Arancel and Cotocoio were added to the ones already mentioned. The track was very heavy due to the rain, so, in their pre-race notes, the trainers preemptively blamed the mud for any potential poor performance. We all know that the condition of the track can affect performance, but before running a Group 1 race that could lead you to the Triple Crown, you shouldn't be looking for excuses. Of course, after they cross the finish line, I will accept and believe all reasons.

Gelsi wasn't a man of excuses. While he acknowledged that his horse wasn't a mud specialist, he told *El País* that good horses win everywhere:

> On a good track, he can't lose, but I don't think he's a mudder. He's perfectly fine, only the track plays against him. We'll discuss it with the owners and Walter. My opinion, I'll say this in advance, is that he should race anyway. A champion has to run on all types of tracks.

The trainer's trust did not extend to the public, who, perhaps dazzled by the colors of La Quebrada or intimidated because Cinzano "wasn't a mudder", favored the Buenos Aires horse Rich Speech and relegated the colt from the stud Valor to second place in the bets. Bettors work in mysterious ways.

The race took place with Label in the lead, stalked by Mogambo, Rich Speech, Cinzano and Capitel. After 300 meters, Cinzano fell to the back as was typical of him, and Mogambo accelerated to take the lead in the race. As they entered the final stretch, Mogambo attempted to break away, but the real action was happening behind, where everything unfolded. One of the most affected was Capitel, who, at around the 500-meter mark, was caught in a domino effect initiated by Dioríssimo on Rich Speech and Amateur, losing all chances.

Walter Báez showed great foresight; he waited for the commotion to settle and, with 300 meters to go, urged Cinzano, who surged forward like a rocket, catching up with Mogambo and beginning to pull ahead. By the time they crossed the finish line, Cinzano had a two-and-a-half-length lead over the second-place horse, which turned out to be Amateur. Mogambo came in third place; Estirado in fourth, and Capitel in fifth place, leaving his entourage with a score to settle. The race time was 1 minute 38.4 seconds, which clearly indicated the poor condition of the track, something the winning jockey made clear to the press:

> I wasn't seeing it as clearly as when he won in 1'29", but I trusted Cinzano's class. He is poised to become this year's champion, because only a truly exceptional horse can win in a track that doesn't suit him, against rivals like those he faced last Sunday.
>
> At the 900-meter mark, he wasn't doing well. Cinzano wanted to run, but he couldn't get a grip. So much so that after the race, he had rubbed off the hair on his pasterns and had some cuts on his legs. All of this happened at the turn. At that point, I thought he wouldn't win. But coming into the final stretch, he settled into his stride. I gave

him a ‘tap’ with the crop, and the horse started running with passion. That's when he showed his great class.

I hadn’t planned on going up the inside; I was going to do whatever I could. I had run the *Polla* before and observed the track was firmer along the rail and about 5 meters outside of it. I notified don Pablo of this detail and we decided to run him a bit off pace and along the rail, waiting for the right moment to make a move. When the ‘mess’ occurred, several horses encountered difficulties. I waited a bit. By then, I was already confident, because Cinzano had shown amazing speeds. That’s when luck came into play, as I found that clear path. I pushed him forward, and he sped past.

I think he is capable of winning the Triple Crown, the only one he might have lost was the *Polla*, because of the distance and the track. Another very good horse would have to come along to beat this one.

I’m very happy because this colt belongs to very good friends, true enthusiasts who are always there.

As it usually happens after a victory in the *Polla*, the hope of having a Triple Crown winner begins to stir; the last one had been Chocón in 1971, the sixteenth horse on the select list, also trained by Pablo Gelsi and ridden by Walter Báez. Every illusion needs to be contrasted with empirical data, esoteric insights, or just talk; anything serves to tone things down and get ready to face a setback because in horse racing, like in all sports, there can only be one winner. So, the first question that comes up after the results of the *Polla* is whether an unlikely horse will 'set the pace' for the winner, to the benefit of another horse eager for revenge after the *Polla.* Another question is whether they 'like the distance', because those extra 400 meters of the *G. P. Jockey Club* have been the downfall of excellent milers. Although, it seems, in the case of Cinzano, this wasn't going to pose any problems. Pablo Gelsi himself would say: "As the distances get longer, it will only get easier." In the same article, the *El País* journalist analyzed the colt's pedigree to confirm the trainer's impression:

> Given the dominance shown last Sunday by the undefeated dark bay, everything suggests that he will indeed be even harder to beat in the future. We are aware of Gelsi's formidable capacity for 'tending' to his protégés.
>
> Without going too far, he worked a miracle with a scrawny filly such as Carelina, daughter of El Carite and granddaughter of Manolo, in which any theory undermined her stamina. What couldn't he do with Cinzano, with a lineage of true stayers? His father, Tudor Park, so far did not excel in producing stayers, but he is the son of Amusette, an exceptional mare who once defeated the best long-distance horses of Maroñas. And his mother, Annabel Lee, produced with Imaginado a notable horse such as Carpintero, winner of one of the races that demand the greatest stamina and endurance in

the entire continent: the *Fuerzas Armadas* over 3200 meters, at the height of La Rinconada. Cinzano certainly has the potential to be a stayer!

Pablo Gelsi and Cinzano after the triumph at the *Polla de Potrillos* (Photo: Facsimile of *El País, cien años en imágenes*).

The *Gran Premio Jockey Club* prize is the second step towards the Triple Crown, the equivalent to the French *Prix du Jockey Club* or the Preakness Stakes in US and disputed one month after the *Polla de Potrillos*. This *Gran Premio* is currently run over 2000 meters, but featured one 2500-meter, four 1750-meter and two 1900-meter editions. The first time it was contested, in 1890, it ended with an unverifiable four-way dead-heat between Ecarte, Indio, Gordon and Kleber. Imperio is included among its first winners, champion of the 1895 edition, which would later turn into the first Uruguayan horse to win a race in the United Kingdom. Few fillies have participated in the race throughout its history, and even fewer have crossed the finish line in triumph—barely seven, the last one being Bakelita, in 1950. From those I was able to watch and not counting *Triple Corona* winners, several stood out among the winners of the *Gran Premio*, such as Mount Royal, Lord Byron—who went on to win stakes in the US—, Quiqueño, Super Cat—the indomitable gray horse from Gavroche—, Rock Ascot—who after one hundred years, once again carried the Uruguayan flag to a British podium—, and Boby di Job, who, on a muddy track, put on a show of speed and agility rarely seen at Maroñas.

Many came seeking revenge at the 1976 Jockey Club; some, like Capitel, due to traffic issues, and others, like Rich Speech, because they were hoping to measure their strengths in a regular track. This appetite for revenge was evident in the pre-race statements of the key players, starting with Fredy Trías:

> Capitel heads for the race in a better condition that before the *Polla* and must display an outstanding performance in any kind of track. He doesn't seem like a specialist in muddy tracks, but he holds his own well. I especially hope that he is not subject to the issues that took away all of his chances at the *Polla*.

Another to speak in advance was Clemente Agüete,

trainer of Rich Speech since the Monday following the *Polla de Potrillos:*

> He's performing much better than on that occasion, and if the track is heavy, I don't think he'll have any problems. What's more: I expect him to justify his trip to Maroñas with a far superior performance. Jockey José Luis Fernández, a filly rider from the Palermo school, will ride him, having already led several horses from the La Quebrada stable to victory.

Genaro Vera's words were premonitory:

> If the track is heavy, as in the Polla, Mogambo will not race. It's another story if the track is 'muddy', and he will be in the race. Of course, I prefer a good track. I see him running the 2'2" distance. He performed very well in the workout. I was completely pleased. I couldn't time the final 200 meters as it was very difficult to gauge the finish from my position. When the commentators informed me that he had completed it in under 12 seconds, I was surprised because he did it without much effort.
>
> If no one makes a move in the race, mine will take care of it. In the *Polla*, he was positioned ahead because I instructed Firpo to run him that way to avoid the common bumps on a very bad track. The horse is in perfect condition and is performing much better than on that occasion.

We'll close the series of articles published by *El País* on the same day as the dispute of the *Gran Premio Jockey Club*, on September 5, 1976, with the words of Pablo Gelsi: "I think he won't lose. I would prefer a good track because he still hasn't given everything he has, because he's a champion."

The trainer had complete faith in the champion, but, as the saying goes, "a race is a race", and, if even Yatasto and Botafogo had lost, why wouldn't Cinzano? A Triple Crown defeat is painful, but it also gives the horse a chance to prove he can overcome adversity, that he doesn't like losing, and that next time, he will give his all to avoid falling behind.

"Hey, you spoiled the result for me!", some centennial might say. Buddy, the race was run forty-five years ago, so that's that. Besides, I was raised in the 20th century, when we would watch movies on TV two years after their cinema release, so I was never one to take the concept of spoilers very seriously.

The colts that participated in Cinzano's first defeat, aside from the ones I previously mentioned, were Amateur, Copón, Engranaje, Fuerte, Lenceo, Scrouchante, the undefeated Plomazo and the Argentine Lord Nelson, who had come in second in the only race he ever disputed in his country, and was here to try his luck against the best Uruguayan generation in the entire decade. In hindsight, we can confirm it probably wasn't the smartest decision.

At the moment of the start, the incident that prevented Cinzano from competing equally for the victory occurred, as he almost fell over. According to Walter Báez, he got 'slayed' at the start and was left with the horse 'trailing through the ground'. The main responsible for the incident was the horse Lord Nelson. This didn't matter much to Jorge Firpo, who had Mogambo run firm in the lead, without paying attention to the harassment inflicted by Rich Speech and Lord Nelson, who had condemned the race of the favorite. The luxurious action of the leader suggested a slow pace of the race, but when he passed the first 1000 meters in one minute, all eyes shifted to the back of the pack, as that split time set the stage for Cinzano's final sprint. But it wasn't so: coming into the stretch, the two Argentines called it quits, one due to exhaustion (Rich Speech), and the other due to an injury. The one who came to challenge the leader was Capitel, but Mogambo still had some reserve left to see him off immediately. In the final 300 meters, the audience exploded, as Cinzano closed to within two lengths of the leader, and everything pointed to a thrilling finish. However, Firpo urged his mount with a couple of strokes of the crop and began to extend his lead again, while Cinzano showed signs of fatigue from the extra effort he had to put in due to the issue at the start. Mogambo finished three and a half lengths ahead at the line, the son of Tudor Park held second place, Capitel came in a solid third, nearly six lengths behind the winner, and Engranaje completed the quartet. The time? Genaro Vera had already foretold it the day before: 2 min 2 s.

Mogambo's victory was so emphatic that the press showered him with well-deserved praise as the new generational star; the great Julio Folle Larreta, known as Doncaster, wrote the following in his column in the newspaper *El País*:

> As before, from Capitel to Cinzano, the crown of the current generation has now passed from Cinzano to Mogambo… and the *Gran Premio Nacional* shall have the last word.
>
> But Mogambo's act at the Jockey Club was dazzling rather than convincing, because of the way he won: with the decisiveness and the luxuries, with the poise of a veritable champion. Skilfully ridden by Jorge Firpo, without hurry or violence, through the gentle 'give and take' of the reins, he softened the horse's natural temper, waited for no one and never relinquished his place of honor. Galloping along—with the benefit of the exceptional length of his stride—he imposed a positively 'crushing' pace to his stride, almost effortlessly.
>
> […]
>
> Capitel caved in before because he attacked first, but eventually Cinzano surrendered as well and bowed his head. And there was definitely no one else but Mogambo in this *Gran Premio Jockey Club*. The Mogambo of the impressive trials. That one that, watching him train, made us think it was impossible for him to ever lose.

Although Cinzano's setbacks had influenced his chances at winning, the display of the chestnut from the Los Nietos stud was such that no one doubted that, on regular conditions, he would also have taken the victory. Los-Kar (another reporter from the time) made it clear that both animals were out of the ordinary, and that their matchup at the *Gran Premio Nacional*, aside from making for a spectacular race, would serve to settle the score:

> ...There are no objections to Mogambo's triumph and we think the vast majority shares this belief. What is indisputable is that we are in the presence of two animals that will honor Uruguayan breeding and racing, and that Cinzano has every right to demand a rematch against the hero of the *Gran Premio Jockey Club*. As is well known, it will take place in the Gran Premio Nacional—which is fast approaching—and that sensational contest will serve to dispel any remaining doubts.

Unfortunately, there was no rematch in the *Gran Premio Nacional*, since a slight health issue (cough) left Mogambo outside of the entries. The *Gran Premio Nacional*, or the *Derby*, as is known in our country, is the last step in the Triple Crown. It takes place one month after the *Gran Premio Jockey Club*, over 2500 meters, and is equivalent to the *Grand Prix de Paris*, which concludes the French Triple Crown or Belmont Stakes in the United States. This race usually establishes the best horse in the generation and, after the Ramírez, must be the competition every owner dreams of winning, as even the tango *Ilusión Burrera* assures: "And although the horse hasn't trained / nor even knows the track yet, / they optimistically dream / of winning the National." It is currently the longest race in the

Uruguayan calendar, since the *Gran Premio de Honor* was lowered from 2800 to 2400 meters. The distance is lava.

In numbers, this race has been somewhat more favorable for fillies than the previous, since thirteen fillies have emerged victorious. The last of them was Glamour, in 1983. The best performance in the modern era was that of La Signora, coming in third after Invasor and Potri Flash, no less. Among the great winners I witnessed who couldn't claim the Triple Crown are Gandhi di Job—who achieved a *double-event* in the *Gran Premio José Pedro Ramírez*—, Viale—who won nine races in the United States between claimings and allowances and still holds the record for 2600 meters at the Hawthorne racetrack—, Lord Byron—whose background in the Jockey Club I have already reviewed—, and the great Redoble, who denied Leicester the Triple Crown two months after finishing second in the *Polla de Potrillos* of Palermo.

Without Mogambo, the race boiled down to a veritable head-to-head between Cinzano and Capitel, with a clear preference for the former, who had just decisively beat the latter in both the *Polla* and the Jockey Club. Other participants were Arlequino, Label—sure to be the pacemaker—, Bluemill—who had just won the Carlos Reyles Stakes over 2300 meters—, El Gatillo, Fratello, Lenceo, Misionero, and Sayón.

Pre-race statements published by *Mundocolor* on November 14 were spicy on both sides, since both Cinzano's and Capitel's supporters were convinced they would win the race. Fredy Trías was perhaps the most careful:

> Now the whole truth will be known. If Cinzano beats mine once again, there will be no more arguing; he is the better one. But we will have to see about that, because I expect Capitel to win. At least, I can assure you he has never been better than now. You'll see the chestnut perform like never before, and the others will need to improve significantly to beat him…

"He has never been better than now", Trías would say, and it was true, because Pedro Hernández's confidence in his mount was amazing:

> Capitel will be hard to beat. He is the colt that appears to be better positioned for the race, and also with extraordinary preparation. On the other hand, he has never done better, and I might add that he is a true stayer, which I don't think his rivals are. They will definitely have to run a lot to beat him.

Pedro, who over time would become one of the best trainers at Maroñas, specializing in long-distance races—those where the trainer's expertise is evident—was decisive. With the bombardment coming from Capitel's camp, Pablo Gelsi couldn't stay behind; after all, his horse was the favorite:

> I believe that I will indeed win the fifth 'derby' because no one can ignore the extraordinary regard I have always had for Cinzano. Now, with the longer distance, I have even more reason to trust him. The colt is in

excellent condition, and something would have to go terribly wrong for him not to win. But, as always, races are races.

There you have it. The stage was set, and the battle of statements gave way to the battle on the track, scheduled for Sunday, November 14, 1976. The race began with the expected leader, Label, at the front. However, after a very slow pace, Walter Báez urged Cinzano on. After crossing the finish line for the first time, he took advantage of the gap left by the leader next to the rails to take the lead in the race. At the "railroad turn", Báez began to increase the pace, which resulted in the first 1000 meters being covered in 1 minute and 4 seconds. This time may seem slow, but considering they ran against the wind and had started the race at a leisurely pace, it can be said that Báez was making his favoritism count. The race was quite boring and with no major variants; Cinzano ahead, flanked by Label, and close by in third, Capitel, until the final 300 meters, when came the adrenaline shot that every horseman anticipates once the entries are known. Label had taken the lead, and Cinzano was pulling away in what seemed like an easy victory. However, Pedro Hernández had saved something for Capitel, and with 200 meters to go, he asked for it, and the horse responded bravely. Báez, warned of the attack, did the same with his, and they locked horns in battle. For a brief moment, the shouts from both camps were justified, but in the final 100 meters, the spectators saw that Cinzano's stamina would prevail over Capitel's tactics. Gelsi's dark bay crossed the finish line more than a length ahead of his rival. The time was 2 minutes 35.6 seconds, an excellent mark that matched the record set by the Triple Crown winner Chocón in 1971, and was the fourth-best time in the last forty-five editions.

Báez and Cinzano, the most successful partnership in 1976.
Photograph: courtesy of Walter Báez.

The victory of Cinzano marked the fifth *Gran Premio Nacional* for Pablo Gelsi, who, by the end of his career, would eventually reach seven wins in this classic race. For his jockey, Walter Báez, it was the fourth derby of seven he would win as jockey, the last one with Maradona, a grey horse trained by Félix Gómez. Known as "*La Fiera*" in Uruguay, Báez also celebrated four additional victories as a trainer and, since he is still active, we hope he adds more jewels to his crown.

The repercussions in the press of this success highlighted Cinzano's virtues but also noted the absence of Mogambo and slightly diminished his victory for two other reasons: the gap left by Arturo Piñeyro, jockey of Label, before entering the "railroad turn", which allowed Báez to take the lead without any issues, and the fact that a trailing horse like him had to set the pace of the race. According to experts, this raised doubts about the stamina of the top two horses. They seemed to disregard the time, because it had been the best record (along with Chocón's) since 1958. Here's an excerpt from what Doncaster published in *El País* the day after the race: An Undisputed Nacional

> Since last Sunday, Maroñas has a new 1976 "Derby Winner". Cinzano, an overwhelming favorite, was the undeniable hero of an undisputed *Gran Premio Nacional*. However, despite tradition's supposed authority, the absence of Mogambo, the brilliant winner of the "Jockey Club," prevents awarding the crown to Cinzano, even though he undeniably claimed the coveted "blue ribbon." We will likely have to wait until the "*Criadores Nacionales*" for the final and definitive verdict.

Meanwhile, in his column "*Desde la Popular*," LosKar wrote the following:

> ...when we regretted Mogambo's withdrawal even more was when the contenders

of the *Gran Premio 'Nacional'* began moving, with an indecisive Label in the lead, closely followed by Cinzano on the inside and Capitel on the outside, both completely restrained by their respective jockeys. It was then that we thought the race was inevitably compromised since its true pace, given a genuinely slow initial speed, was significantly reduced, and in this way, the true stamina and outstanding quality that could be attributed to both Cinzano and Capitel could not emerge at all.

With this victory, Cinzano becomes the best of the year—having won two of the races that make up the 'Triple Crown'—but his showdown with Mogambo remains pending, and the question lingers: What would have happened if Genaro Vera's pupil had taken part in the great race? It cannot be said he would have won, but the race would certainly would have played out differently.

With these doubts about their potential, both Cinzano and Capitel faced each other in the Gran Premio Criadores Nacionales, a 2500-meter race held two weeks after the Derby, which would also feature two supporting actors: Moratín and Fratello.

On November 28, the two colts faced each other again to settle something that, for everyone except Capitel's supporters, was already decided. Knowing that the other two rivals were not even a threat, they started the race head-to-head from the beginning, Capitel on the inside rail and Cinzano close beside him, on the second lane. Fratello positioned himself two lengths behind, while Moratín lagged more than 50 meters from the main action, hoping to snatch second place if either of the favorites tired. Up to the 1000-meter mark, the race was even. But then Báez pushed the pace slightly and took the lead. Pedro urged Capitel to keep up, but as they entered the final straight, the horse from the Godoy stud got tough in Durán's way and said, "No mas." From that moment, the race turned into an exhibition, and Cinzano became a freight train. Free of his opponent, he began to pull further ahead, crossing the finish line with a ten-length lead over Moratín, who, at the last moment, overtook Capitel for second place. The race time was 2 minutes 36 seconds and 3/5, and the manner in which the champion reached the finish cleared up any doubts that may have lingered from the Jockey Club race. There was less talk of Mogambo, despite his absence from this race as well. The next meeting between the two titans would not be until January 6, 1977, in the 2800-meter *Gran Premio José Pedro Ramírez*, the premier event in Uruguayan horse racing.

The Ramírez pays tribute to the first president of the Uruguayan Jockey Club and began its journey as an International Grand Prize. Traditionally, it is run on January 6th and marks the end of the Uruguayan turf season. Its first edition took place in 1889 over a distance of 3500 meters and was won by the French horse Havre. The first Uruguayan victory was achieved by Imperio in 1897, when the race was already being run over 3000 meters. The distance has varied over time, and since 1981, it covers 2400 meters. Historically, the race has been dominated by Argentine and Uruguayan horses, although in the 21st century (especially in the last decade), Brazilian-born horses have taken the spotlight. The horses that have won the race more than once are Amsterdam, Buen Ojo, ¡Socorro!, Romántico, Sestao, Hielo, and Gandhi di Job, all with two victories. Buen Ojo and Sestao are the only ones who did not achieve their wins consecutively. This race is also one of four required to win the "Quadruple Crown," a title awarded to the triple-crowned colt that also wins the Ramírez. There have been few quadruple-crowned winners throughout history: Sisley (who also holds an unparalleled record, having won the Argentine National and the Uruguayan National a week apart), Romántico, Bizancio, and Amodeo, who became the last quadruple-crowned winner to date with his victory in the 1989 Ramírez. A necessary clarification: neither Invasor nor Sir Fever ran the Ramírez because they were exported beforehand; surely, both would have achieved the feat, but the "what ifs" do not make history, they only spark heated conversations at bar tables.

Things didn't look good for Cinzano before the race, as his usual jockey, Walter Báez, was serving a severe disciplinary suspension. Thus, Cinzano would have to debut a new jockey in none other than the premier race of Uruguayan horse racing. The chosen one was Carlos Gómez, a great rider of the time who, later in 1980, would win the first edition of the *Revancha del Ramírez* at the *Hipódromo Real de San Carlos de Colonia* on the horse Cyndello. In addition to the jockey change, the list of participants was much more challenging than in his last two victories; there were plenty of horses with credentials that would intimidate anyone, starting with his stablemate, the gray Max (Lennox and Marca), who had recently performed outstandingly in Brazil and won four consecutive stakes at Maroñas. Anyone wanting to win the Ramírez would have to beat him.

Among the colts, the most formidable rival was Mogambo, his only conqueror up to that point, who had reappeared a month before this race in the *Clásico Comparación*, finishing four lengths behind Max and Chasqueado in a sensational 2 minutes 33 seconds for the 2500 meters. The other participating colts were Capitel, seeking redemption, with the international Julio Fajardo confirmed as his rider; Moratín; and the Argentine Crest Pan (Snow Crest and Zum), who had finished second in the *Polla de Potrillos* at Palermo and had won the *Gran Premio Jockey Club* also at Palermo. Although he had recently failed in the *Gran Premio Nacional*, he was a very dangerous rival. The rest of the field included Uleanto and Adriatic. The former was a Brazilian horse with eleven career wins in his country, including the *Derby Paulista* and the *Grande Prêmio Bento Gonçalves*. His most recent achievement was a win on December 26, 1976, just two weeks before the race, at the *Hipódromo Cristal de Porto Alegre*. Adriatic was a horse that was a few steps below all the aforementioned horses and would later become one of the best sires of the late 20th century in Uruguay.

Conmemorative painting of the 1977 Ramírez. Photo: courtesy of Walter Báez.

The two press favorites, Max and Cinzano, were under the command of Pablo Gelsi, who, as if he could see the future, declared this to *Mundocolor*:

> It's a race that will be worth watching. There are several very good horses that ought to put on a great show. My protégés are two of the main contenders. In fact, they might even decide the race between them. Both need to improve on their last performances, as they are better prepared than they were then. Honestly, I can’t say that one is better than the other. I’ve never compared them directly. Both are also running like never before. I don’t know how far they’ll go... I see them as very evenly matched, and if that’s the case, the

> circumstances might determine the result in favor of one or the other. Sincerely, I think that's how it will be...

As always, when a foreign horse steps onto Maroñas to compete with ours, all eyes are on him; Crest Pan was no exception, and his trainer, Saturnino Bello, had to face the microphones before the race:

> Crest Pan is doing very well, despite the many hours of travel, and I hope that on Thursday he performs well enough to add excitement to the big race.
>
> It's not true that he was unwell for the Gran Premio Nacional; that was an invention of the press. If he hadn't been well, it would have been illogical to run him. He was boxed in throughout the race. When he needed to improve, Jara had no choice but to pull up and go around several horses. That's where he lost all his chances. For this race, his workouts have left me very satisfied. Two days ago, he did 1200 in 1'15" in great form, in La Plata.

Thursday, January 6 arrived, and, just like on the day of the *Polla de Potrillos*, the public placed their bets on the foreigner. To everyone's surprise, Crest Pan garnered 23,591 tickets, compared to Max's 13,142 and Cinzano's 11,870. In today's terms, the Argentine horse paid 1.80, Max 2.90, and the champion 3.20. With this scenario on the boards, the horses began to settle into the starting gates. A nervous silence spread among the crowd, quickly followed by the explosive start of the race.

Mogambo took the lead with authority, but Max immediately went to challenge him; a length behind were Adriatic and Crest Pan; close to them was Cinzano, followed by Uleanto and Moratín, with Capitel bringing up the rear. An ear-splitting roar accompanied the first pass in front of the stands and the entry into the "railroad turn", from which they emerged into the backstretch as a very compact group, with no changes in positions. The moderate pace (1000 meters in 1 minute 2 seconds and 1/5) forced the jockeys to work hard, unable to play with the the tempo of the race and having to focus on a smooth run because none of the front-runners were burning excessive energy. From the 1200-meter mark, Jorge Firpo attempted a breakaway with Mogambo, and the race took on a dizzying pace, difficult to match even in today's 2400-meter races. For reference, they ran those last 1200 meters in 1 minute 12 seconds and 3/5. Firpo tried to settle the race in the final turn, but this time he had a great one like Max, ridden by Cleber Sanguinetti, who wasn't going to lose ground. Midway through the curve, the difference between the two was less than a length; Adriatic raised the white flag and dropped out of the race; Uleanto, visibly stretched, struggled against the inevitable; Moratín gave hope, and Cinzano moved up more comfortably with the leaders. Meanwhile, the Chilean Eduardo Jara felt the pressure of being the outsider, as they boxed Crest

Pan in, reducing his chances to almost none; in last place, with more patience than Kung Fu, Julio Fajardo held on with Capitel.

Entering the final straight, several horses still had a chance. Mogambo's prospects expired with 400 meters to go, when he was overtaken by Max, who now had to fend off his stablemate, Cinzano, who, driven by Carlos Gómez, caught up with 300 meters remaining and passed him with 200 meters left, although the dapple-gray horse refused to give up. While all eyes were on Gelsi's steeds, Capitel started to make a surprising run at the *Folle Stand*, causing the crowd to roar. One furlongs from the finish, he was two and a half lengths behind Cinzano, and with 100 meters to go, he had closed the gap to just over a length and was running the fastest of the three. With 50 meters left, Cinzano led Max by a quarter length and Capitel by three-quarters, thrilling the few who had bet on him (he paid 21-1). But the finish line is always in the same place, and Tudor Park's son managed to hold off the challenge, maintaining the lead over Max, who in turn kept Fajardo's horse at bay by half a neck. Mogambo finished fourth, two lengths behind, and Moratín came fifth in a respectable race. The race time was a marvelous 2 minutes 52 seconds and 3/5, unimaginable today, especially considering that this distance is no longer run.

This time, all the journalists acknowledged Cinzano's quality. He had bravely defeated the best adult horse in Uruguay, who that season had competed in Brazil's most important stakes, finishing third in the *Grande Prêmio Brasil* (La Gávea), third in the *Grande Prêmio São Paulo* (Cidade Jardim), and second in the *Grande Prêmio Bento Gonçalves* (Cristal), all Group 1 races. As if that weren't enough, he also defeated the two best three-year-olds of his generation, leaving the last *Bento Gonçalves* winner ten lengths behind and the last *Gran Premio Jockey Club* winner at the *Hipódromo Argentino de Palermo* fifteen lengths behind. Let's review what Mundocolor published the next day:

> [Max] is the true and consecratory measure for a colt like Cinzano. To beat Max, it wasn't enough to be the best of the year; you had to be a true champion...
>
> Cinzano was the winner of a race that had enormous prestige, due to the level of the race and the beautiful scenarios it presented throughout. Tudor Park's son ran in intermediate positions while the pace was set evenly by Mogambo asking for rein and Max following him with his characteristic and unwavering tenacity.
>
> Cinzano confirmed his powerful spurt when, in the final straight, he was upon them in four strides. And he then confirmed his bravery when he had to face the expected resistance from the dapple-gray horse. It proved once again that 'for every brave one, there's always another brave one.' Max found that in his own stablemate, and despite fighting with all his might, he couldn't counter the colt's push.

> But if from the final 400 meters the contest was exciting to the highest degree, the crowd had to feel even greater suspense—and here it could truly be said that it reached the point of drama—when Capitel appeared in a furious rush. It seemed incredible to think that those two brave, all-heart, all-quality horses could be relegated at the final stage. But like a whirlwind, there was Capitel, with strength, with fury, with a rebellion over his recent failures, as if saying that he definitely belonged among the greats of a magnificent generation. Those final, decisive meters were among the best in the rich and long history of our premier horseracing event.

With Cinzano's triumph came the first offers, but none were attractive enough to make the horse leave Gelsi's stables. However, Mogambo did leave the Maroñas stables after the big race. The son of Ujier was sold to Brazil and would go on to defend the colors of *Haras Santa Ana do Rio Grande*, but it would not be a farewell, as fate would bring them face to face once more on Brazilian soil, as we will see later.

Cinzano's next appearance was on Sunday, March 13, just over two months after his Ramírez victory. The race was the *Gran Premio Municipal*, run over 2400 meters, and among his rivals was once again Capitel, who had a 0-4 record against Gelsi's champion. However, except for the *Criadores Nacionales*, Capitel had always run well enough to deserve a rematch; although when there are many rematches without changing the result, we would be allowed to go to the barn and say: “Come on, my friend.” The rest of the rivals were far below the level of these two colts: Chasqueado, once a good horse, was on the decline; El Caburé was a good miler; and Ormolo, Amateur; Misionero and Sayón had backgrounds that didn’t pose a threat to anyone.

Pablo Gelsi, Carlos Gómez and Cinzano wave at the crowds after winning the Ramírez Cup (Photography: copy of *El País* newspaper, courtesy of Luis Costa Baleta).

The race was a formality, another “easy win” for Cinzano, who defeated Capitel by more than four lengths, with El Caburé completing the trifecta. The time was nothing extraordinary, 2 minutes 29.4 seconds, and the highlight of the race was Walter Báez’s return to the saddle after his suspension.

There was no doubt that Cinzano was the best horse in Uruguay, and at that time, the best were going to challenge the best in Brazil. So, they booked tickets to the northern country with the goal of winning the *Grande Prêmio São Paulo*, a Group 1 race over 2400 meters held in Cidade Jardim, which in the 1976 edition had seen Max contesting the race, without success.

Cinzano, the day before the *G. P. São Paulo*. Photo: *Folha do São Paulo*.

The trip went smoothly, but problems began in the preparation for the race: an error in the horse's shoeing caused him to develop laminitis and had to run with a special fiberglass shoe. In a race like this, you cannot afford any disadvantages, and Cinzano was already at a disadvantage before the start. This was significant considering that, besides the Brazilian star Agente, winner of the 1976 *Derby Paulista*, there were Paris, the best Argentine horse (winner of the *Polla* in Palermo, second in the *Jockey Club*, and second in the *Nacional*), and his only conqueror so far: Mogambo.

On May 1, 1977, the rain was pouring down on São Paulo, but the stands were still packed. At that time, horse racing in Brazil was still the second most popular sport after football. Today, Brazilian horse racing continues to produce quality horses (only Argentina can compete with them), but it has never regained the popular support it had back then.

The rain had eased a bit when the starter positioned himself for the start of the race. One by one, the fifteen participants took their places, and a few minutes later, fourteen heads emerged in pursuit of victory. Fourteen? Yes, the fifteen were completed by Cinzano, who had a delayed start. If the challenge was already difficult with the shoe problem, this delay made his victory seem like a mirage. As expected, Mogambo set the pace and controlled the field; anyone wanting to win the trophy would have to take it from him, which was understood perfectly by Agente's jockey, who engaged in a struggle from the first 200 meters to defend the local horse's honor. As they passed the finish line for the first time, Mogambo, ridden by Adaíl Oliveira, quickened the pace and pulled four lengths ahead of his pursuer. Meanwhile, Cinzano was at the back, several lengths behind after a poor start and a subsequent disturbance caused by the loss of position from several horses when he tried to catch up with the pack. As they turned into the backstretch, Roberto Penacchio urged his horse to close the gap Mogambo had created, so the lead was again shared between the Uruguayan and Agente. The rest of the competitors were several lengths behind the leaders, while Cinzano trailed far behind, with Walter Báez trying every possible way to get the horse into the race. A new downpour fell on the racetrack, significantly reducing visibility, making it hard for the crowd at Cidade Jardim to clearly see the competitors. As they began to turn the last bend, to the surprise and admiration of the crowd, Mogambo made another burst and opened up several lengths on Agente, who no longer had the strength to fight head-to-head. Among the rest, the only one who seemed determined to contest was the Argentine Paris, who, turning with a wide angle in the form of a fan, gained positions from the back. And at the back was Cinzano, now closing the gap at mid-field. When he had passed four rivals, he encountered an equine barrier, so his jockey had to slow down and widen his line, losing time and position compared to the two leaders. As they entered the final stretch, Agente made one last effort and, driven by his champion's pride, caught up with Mogambo, but his task was done. The chestnut was running at a relentless pace, as if born to run on grass. But all effort requires energy, and Mogambo's was starting to wane; he had been running non-stop for 2100 meters, and the last 300 meters would seem eternal. To make matters worse, the Gotacha silks were advancing wide. "Paris *viejo nomás*, Pezoa *viejo nomás*," the Argentines shouted to encourage the horse bred in La Quebrada, while further back Cinzano was passing rivals as if he were a Formula 1 car, but it seemed he wouldn't have enough stretch to fight for the win. With great courage and quality, Mogambo defended his position until the very finish line, crossing a nose ahead of Paris; third, coming from the back, was the veteran Arnaldo; fourth was Agente, and fifth, three lengths behind the winner, was Cinzano, who fought with Paris for the prize of "who gave away more of the race" .

The Brazilians were so surprised by Mogambo's victory that *Folha do São Paulo* headlined, "No one expected such a victory," even mistakenly stating in the report that he had always lost to Cinzano and that many present were surprised to learn that his jockey, Adaíl Oliveira, was a Gaúcho and not Uruguayan. The journalist, historian, and writer Miguel Aguirre Bailey was at Cidade Jardim that Workers' Day and, in an article published by La Biblia Burrera titled "Mogambo was the winner… but Cinzano…," wrote the following:

> At both ends, the two Uruguayan steeds — Mogambo and Cinzano — with the same colors but different designs on their silks, had played their cards. The balance tipped in favor of the striking chestnut, who achieved an exceptional victory, leaving the noble bay with all the responsibility of 'making up for lost time'… striving for a victory that was practically

> unattainable from the start. Mogambo was a legitimate winner…, but Cinzano proudly maintained his best credentials.

Aguirre Bailey, in the book "*Walter Báez: 'El Justiciero'*, " comments on this race: "In over fifty years of watching horse racing, rarely have we seen such an unjust defeat as Cinzano's in Brazil. But races… are races."

Upon returning from the trip, there was a lucrative offer for the son of Tudor Park: Mr. Luis Donamarí, a trainer and intermediary of the time, had offered $80,000 for the horse, an amount impossible to refuse at that time. The destination seemed to be the United States, with the trip scheduled for early June if the sale was confirmed. The horse had been inspected by an American woman with two Argentine veterinarians, who gave their approval. After the transaction was completed, the horse was moved to Donamarí's stud, where it would await all necessary documentation for export. Although the amount was extraordinary, exporting racehorses was not unusual as these exports were one of the most significant sources of income in the Uruguayan horse racing industry. What was unusual was that the traveling companion was Lebón, a son of Lemmy from the Caraguatá stud (founded in 1950 by Cyro Mattos Moglia), who had shown precocity but, at five years old, was closer to heading off to an equine therapy center than continuing to compete on the racetracks. Perhaps the woman and the veterinarians had seen something that the Uruguayans had not, but it remained implausible that this horse was also being exported to the United States. The doubt was planted in the Uruguayan horse racing world and would later blossom into an unprecedented investigation, but at the time, it was just another detail among many. What mattered was the sale of Cinzano; the Uruguayan horse racing dream machine was in motion: the champion would go on to prove his worth at American racetracks.

CONVICT

THE VOYAGE

The horse arrived in the United States along with Lebón, Boots Colonero (an undefeated Argentine horse) and six other Argentine horses, all of them purchased by Mark Gerard (the main character in this story), the veterinarian of Secretariat and Kelso, among other great champions.

Mark Joel Geronimus was born on October 6, 1934, in Brooklyn, New York. He studied veterinary medicine at Cornell University, and, after graduating, changed his name (how could we miss this sign?) to Mark Gerard, although everyone called him Mike. When he was ten years old, his sister gave him a retired polo horse, which marked the start of a never-ending love of horses. During his stay at Cornell University College of Veterinary Medicine, he was captain of the polo team, with which he earned several trophies.

Over the holidays, he worked as an exercise rider at the New York racetracks; this got him acquainted with Sunny Jay Fitzsimmons, who trained the Phipps family horses. From this point on, a combination of connections and talent would take care of the rest. Demanding when it came to work, he was charismatic, having built his way up and forging an ability to relate amicably with people from all walks of life. According to those who met him in his trips to the Rio de la Plata, he was a true gentleman, very capable in his equestrian activities, and flawless on a personal level. This remained true until September 23, 1977, when a victory that was supposed to go unnoticed did anything but, in the newsroom of a newspaper in a country too small to be a concern.

Back to the voyage, we get the first hint of obscurity, since, upon making a stopover in Panama, the nationality of the horse from La Plata, Boots Colonero, was changed to Panamanian according to his new documents. This is how two Uruguayan horses and one horse from Panama officially made it to New York, as described in the November 14, 1977 edition of *Sports Illustrated*: "The flight, also carrying six Argentine horses, made a stopover at the Tocumen Airport in Panama, to load the horse Boots Colonero, whom Gerard also bought."

Upon arriving at the airport, on June 4, 1977, the three horses were put under mandatory quarantine by the Department of Agriculture, where blood tests were performed and all the corresponding veterinary examinations were carried out. The three arrived without an identifying picture, but the Uruguayans at least had a record, prepared and presented to the authorities by the intermediary, as was required by the thoroughbred importation regulations at that time, as there was no actual communication between Jockey Clubs. Lebón's record described him as a five-year-old bay stallion with a white star on his forehead; Cinzano's record noted he, too, was a four-year-old bay stallion with a white star on his forehead and a scar a couple of centimeters long on his left shoulder.

After completing the seventy-two-hour quarantine, Boots Colonero was shipped westbound, where he was registered to the name of Daniel Agnew; in turn, the Uruguayans left for Muttontown Farm, Gerard's estate in Long Island, where they would begin their adaptation to the new setting. Lebón, who had been purchased for $1600 in Uruguay, was "sold" to Jack P. Morgan for $10,000; in turn, Cinzano, who had been acquired for $81,000, was sold for $150,000 to tycoon Joseph Taub, who at the time owned the New Jersey Nets—among other things—, an NBA franchise based in Brooklyn since 2012.

Jack P. Morgan was a Vietnam War veteran who had received a bronze medal for his bravery. Following in the footsteps of his father, he dedicated himself to training racehorses, putting his knowledge of the local scene in Belmont Park to good use. But, ever since Lebón's "purchase", the odds seemed to be consistently against him. Naively enough, the trainer had agreed to Dr. Gerard's request to act as Lebón's owner to avoid compromising him professionally—in the State of New York, veterinarians cannot own race horses.

But perhaps this is just a facade: as we'll see, in all his appearances, Morgan consistently tries to soften our hearts with his apparent innocence or lack of insight, but all his moves are made in pursuit of his own benefit. Deep down, he knew that if he was successful with someone as famous as Gerard, his stocks would go up and other owners would come knocking on his door. What could actually go wrong? Spoiler alert: Everything.

Good ol' Jack continued caring for horses, but he never had much support or success after September 23, 1977. His high point would come fifteen years later, at Belmont Park, when his pupil (and the only horse he was training back then), Shining Bid, won the True North Handicap (Group 2) with a payout of 30-1.

THE ACCIDENT

Once the transactions were confirmed, all that was left to do was comply with the mandatory quarantine at Gerard's farm. But on the night of June 12, barely eight days after the horses arrived on U.S. soil, the accident occurred in which Cinzano lost his life. It appears that a few cats and a rabbit were running around in the stable, the horse got scared, reared up, and hit his head, causing a fracture. When it all happened, Gerard was having dinner at Frank Wright's home, and, when he got the call, went back to his farm right away. Before leaving, he asked his host if he could send one of the guests to the estate if he didn't return, as he would need a witness. It was Wright himself who went over to Gerard's house, to find a dead horse in one of the stalls. In order to be able to receive the insurance payment, it was necessary to have the horse's death confirmed by a different veterinarian. Gerard called his friend and colleague Harry Hemphill, who, without seeing the body, ratified everything that Gerard had told him over the phone in a certificate.

The news quickly reached newsrooms in Uruguay, but with few details to spare. The surprise was so great and the details surrounding the death of an unknown thoroughbred in the U.S. were so scarce, that journalists had to rely on their imagination to fill in the informational gaps. For instance, in the first article published by "La Mañana", the only accurate information was the fact of the horse's death and the location of the injuries.

> When the truck that was transporting him to Belmont Park in the United States, crashed—after completing his "quarantine"—the "champion" Cinzano had to be put down. A severe fracture in one of his legs and a serious head injury led those responsible for his care to make the painful decision. Tudor Park's son had been recently purchased by the well-known TV and film actor Telly Savalas (Kojak), for $81,000.

When I read this, I understood why every time the subject of Cinzano would come up in conversation, my father used to say: "He belonged to Kojak, that bald guy from TV, remember?" Regardless of the fact that later on everyone refuted this information, the Mandela Effect had already taken hold in the mind of my old man. The "truck accident" mentioned in the first paragraph could very well have been part of the official communication from Mark Gerard's circle mentioned as part of the cover-up, and the thing about Telly Savalas being the owner sounds more like a cinematographic twist from a journalist, who, aside from informing and keeping his readers hooked, had to navigate the communicational limitations of the time.

THE RESURRECTION

After Cinzano's death was confirmed, the Uruguayan horse racing world moved on and continued with business as usual. News from America only made it to Uruguay through the occasional journalist or an international news agency reporting on a major race. Because of this, Lebón's arrival to Jack Morgan's stud at Belmont Park went unnoticed, even more so taking into account that Mrs. Gerard had bought him for personal use and not for competition, so no one was keeping track of his whereabouts. According to Morgan, the horse was very thin and out of form when he arrived, with little appetite and complaining of pain in his right fetlock, although he quickly regained his competitive condition. Dr. Gerard had told him that Lebón was a much better horse than his record indicated, so the prospect of winning a few races excited Jack Morgan, who had fewer than ten horses in his care.

FIFTH—$9,500; Clmg; ($12,500—$10,500); 3-up; 1⅛ m. T.—:23⅘, :46⅘, 1:11⅗, 1:38, 1:44⅗. Off—3:36 Winner—Belrose Farm's—B. g. 7, by Graphic—Reterkopf.

Horses	Wt.	P.P.	St.	½	Str.	Fin.	Jockeys	St.	Pl.	Sh.	Eq.Odds
M-12-Mr. Champ	119	12	8	7½	1¼	1 1¼	Cordero	$12.60	6.00	4.00	$ 5.20
B-2-PlayTheM'ket	117	2	3	2 1½	2½	2hd	Cauthen	—	7.00	6.20	8.10
F-6-El Sin Rival	117	6	7	8 1½	3 1	3 1¾	Adams	—	—	5.20	8.60
Ventorillo	117	11	1	3½	5½	4¾	Venezia	—	—	—	13.80
Fast And Evil	117	10	11	5 1	6 2	5¾	Maple	—	—	—	16.10
Surf	117	8	2	9 1½	7 1	6¾	Hernandez	—	—	—	7.50
Finney Finster	117	3	10	11 4	9 4	7nk	Vasquez	—	—	—	15.50
Doubt	117	5	4	4½	4hd	8 1½	Santiago	—	—	—	22.00
Proud Romeo	117	1	5	1hd	8½	9 1¼	Turcotte	—	—	—	6.00
Rock Dancer	117	4	9	12	10½	10nk	Velasquez	—	—	—	11.00
Lebon	113	7	12	10½	11 3	11 1½	Wallis	—	—	—	7.40
Minstrel II	113	9	6	6 2	12	12	Pla	—	—	—	5.80

SCR:—**Li'l Tommie (H), Cut The Talk (N).**

EXACTA—12(M)-2(B) PAID $53.20

OTB—M—$11.80 5.60 3.80; B—6.60 5.80; F—4.80. EXACTA (M-B) PAID $50.40

Results of Lebón's debut in the United States (*Daily News* facsimile).

Lebón's first race in the United States took place on September 9, 1977, in a claiming race with a $9,500 purse over 1,800 meters. With no notable rivals (one of them being the Argentine Minstrel II), and with unremarkable performances in Uruguay, the 15-1 morning line odds quickly became 55-1. While waiting for the race to start, Morgan placed a $10 bet on Lebón, if for nothing else, as a way to show support for his horse. With just two minutes remaining before the betting closed, the unexpected happened: Lebón's odds dropped from 50-1 to 7-1. The trainer was at a loss, "Maybe someone knows something I don't", he thought, and put in an additional $10. Afterwards, it was revealed that a mysterious woman had placed a $10,000 bet on Lebón. That same afternoon, ridden by B. L. Willis, the horse did not perform well, and finished second to last, sixteen lengths behind the winner. At least he beat the Argentine horse...

Lebón kept improving his athletic condition and on Friday, September 23, he got the unlikely chance of improving his debut and latest performances at Maroñas with an unprecedented (for him) 2000 meters on grass. The race was a claiming race with a $10,000 purse, and the morning line had him at 20-1. At that moment, no one thought that this race would change the life of so many people, one horse, and the way imported horses are identified in the U.S. The trainer, true to his habit of supporting his charges, placed a few dollars on him to win and wasn't surprised to see the payout of 116.00 on the tote board. But he was indeed surprised when he kept gaining ground in the final stretch, in a scene that could have been taken from the show *Seconds from Disaster.* Thus, number two, Lebón, with Larry Adams in the saddle, crossed the finish line four lengths ahead of Li'l Tommie, an eight-year-old ridden by the legend Laffit Pincay Jr., who until then had seven victories and a fourth place in the Dixie Handicap (Group 2). Georgetown came in third, a three-year-old maiden who would come to win five races and earn just over $100,000 in prize money; he was also ridden by a legend: Jorge Velásquez. The time of the race was 2 min 5 s for two kilometers, and the juicy part of the rainy afternoon was the payouts: 116.00 for the win, 60.00 for place, and 16.80 for show; the trifecta paid (wait for it) 29,855 dollars per ticket.

It is likely that the 12,115 individuals who were there that afternoon left Belmont with their jaws dropped, ignoring they would become part of 20th-century horse racing history. They were also unaware that, just like thc loaves of bread in the story of Jesus, they would multiply over the years: if one were to follow the stories that circulated during the 80s, that day, over 200,000 people had gone to the racetrack.

The news of Lebón's victory in the United States reached our country and was met with astonishment—in theory, the horse had been taken there for rides and equestrian activities. The surprise was such that Cyro Mattos Moglia, his former owner, was having lunch in his usual table at the Maroñas racetrack and, when they told him Lebón had won in the U.S. in a 2000-meter race, he shot right away: "That is not Lebón." From experience, he knew the horse could not run beyond 1300 meters. Mr. Mattos' disbelief was shared by the entire horse racing community when the cable from the news agency became known. In addition to the distance, it indicated that the victory had been on turf. When the telephoto was sent to the newsrooms of *Mundocolor* and *El País,* journalists confirmed the response from the former owner: that horse was not Lebón.

"Lebón" at the podium after his victory at Belmont Park. Photo: *Rice's Derby Choice Journal* 2013.

But who was Lebón? A son of Lemmy and Talavera who had been born in 1972 in the fields of Haras San Miguel and whom Cyro Mattos had chosen with his usual good eye, as he looked for precociousness and speed for an affordable price. He had undoubtedly achieved his goal with this horse, who, trained by the memorable Antonio Marsiglia, was undefeated in his first three races held in 1975 and even achieved a stakes win. But Lebón's prowess had an expiration date, and immediately after that triumph, he started a *moonwalking* stage that would have no end. According to Álvaro Mattos, Cyro's son, "he was a very limited horse," a fact confirmed by his record at Maroñas: four wins in thirteen races, with three of those achieved in his first three races, two years before being sold. When Gerard's wife chose him, she surprised the father as much as the son, since the intermediary told them he would be used for equestrian activities:

> That's when we exchanged glances with my dad because the horse wasn't fit for equestrian activities. He had a very athletic physique—slim, tall—so it didn't quite make sense to us that he would be selected to perform equestrian activities, where, as far as I understand, they look for more harmonious, large, powerful horses.

Once they got over the initial surprise, the owner asked what they were offering. When he heard it was $1600, he didn't hesitate for a moment: the market value wasn't more than $1000 for a horse of this type. Continuing with the words of Alvaro Mattos, he stated he always wondered why Lebón had been chosen:

> We heard the horse had been shipped to the U.S. along with Cinzano. And, while it was possible the horses had the same review, the same

whorls and the same markings, someone must have studied them, because Cinzano was shorter, more robust, whereas this one was slender, taller, and completely different in morphological terms. Even the color was different, Cinzano was a black bay, while Lebón was a lighter bay, with unremarkable hair—he wasn't a pretty or striking horse. We never put him up for sale, the offer came on its own and my dad didn't hesitate for one second to take it. After the fact gained notoriety, we would tease him together with Marsiglia, telling him he must have taken a share from the people who made the switch in the U.S.

If there's one thing this story has taught me (and I apologize for bringing it up now instead of in the prologue) is that each person who is interviewed, each source that is reviewed, has their own version—this is a wonderful thing. The race Cinzano won was the second he ever ran, but, depending on who is reporting, it was either the first or the third; the actual distance was 2000 meters, but can vary from a mile to 2400 meters according to the source; the actual cause of death was an accident at the farm, but I have heard and read everything from murder, to the first version reported by *El País,* which mentioned a truck accident. Álvaro Mattos himself even stated that the death occurred during a train accident while the horse was being transported to the farm. The only detail they all agree on is that the race he won was run on grass.

THE INVESTIGATION

While in Uruguay, investigations into the alleged fraud began under the leadership of journalists Julián Pérez and Daniel Rodríguez Oteiza, the 'star' (?) Lebón continued his training, unaware of what was about to unfold. On October 12, he ran what would be his last official race at the Meadowlands Racetrack in New Jersey, where the main events are harness races, though each fall it opens its track to thoroughbreds. The race was an allowance with a $20,000 purse, run on grass over 1,800 meters, and Lebón was not among the favorites. The final odds were 14.90, but he only managed to finish fourth, several lengths behind the winner, Faithful Diplomat, a fine horse with 12 wins in 75 starts and some involvement in group stakes races. If one looks at the race chart and sees that with 400 meters to go he was trailing far behind, one might guess that, just like in his debut, he was set up to fail, and his closing speed wasn't enough to make the board. The jockey was once again Larry Adams, another figure who would eventually show up in the crime reports—because no one got away clean here, they were all in on it, from the owner to the jockey.

A few days before the race, Julián Pérez published an

article in *Mundocolor* in which he ventured a hypothesis that would turn out to be correct:

> While there is a lack of concrete data on the matter—something that would prove to be dramatic if confirmed—there are a few points that, through very simple deductions, suggest a potential scheme. These points are the following: 1) Lebón, a horse with a very promising start on the tracks, remaining undefeated in his first three appearances, later showed a noticeable decline until being auctioned off at the Maroñas paddock for the insignificant sum of N$ 3,800. 2) A few days after being auctioned, Lebón was purchased for a significantly higher amount, for purposes of being exported to the United States. 3) Lebón was shipped on the same plane as Cinzano. 4) The two animals are physically very different. Lebón is larger and has a darker coat than the "star" Cinzano. However, both have a similar marking on their foreheads. 5) Cinzano dies, and Lebón, showing a remarkable improvement in performance, debuts with a "spectacular" win, competing at a distance for which, like most of his paternal siblings, he had not demonstrated good aptitude at Maroñas.

On Thursday, October 20, six days after Pérez and Rodríguez Oteiza's call to the Jockey Club in the United States, a wire from the Associated Press mentioned that the NYRA (New York Racing Association) was investigating an accusation made by Uruguayan journalists who claimed that the horse named Lebón was actually Cinzano and that documentation confirming this was being sent from Uruguay. What evidence would be sent by post from Uruguay? The official records of the horses, supplied by the Montevideo Jockey Club. Meanwhile, the horse's handlers, unaware of what was coming, pre-registered Lebón to race on Saturday, October 22, at the Meadowlands Racetrack. It came as a surprise to all the journalists that, after finishing a distant fourth in an allowance race, Lebón was enrolled in the Nelson Handicap against his three previous victors. Due to the ongoing investigation, the authorities banned the horse from participating in the race and also removed him from the Meadowlands Cup, scheduled for Saturday, October 29, in which the horse had also been pre-enrolled. If people were surprised by his entry in a handicap race, imagine the reaction when they saw him as a potential participant in a stakes race with a $150,000 purse.

On Friday, October 21, after the information from the Uruguayan journalists arrived, the U.S. Jockey Club was ready to begin the investigation. However, the process could not commence immediately because "the Jockey Club offices close on weekends," so they had to wait until Monday to receive further updates.

In Uruguay, the investigation that began after Lebón's victory was relentless. They were searching for information everywhere, leaving no stone unturned, no matter how tiny, and interviewing everyone connected to Cinzano. Onc of those interrogated was his former owner, Roberto Forné, who, speaking in the aftermath of the victory and with the official investigation still in its early stages, gave some rather colorful statements to the newspaper *El País*.

He kicked off the interview with a bang: "I would recommend not sending anyone to investigate over there: if it's true that a massive fraud involving astounding sums has been orchestrated, I don't think the person sent would come back alive." After such a bold statement, he moderated his approach and said something that more or less captured the sentiment of all Uruguayan horseracing fans:

> "I think it would be very good for breeding if Cinzano, even under a different name, were still alive. He's an extraordinary horse, who had only completed the first eight months of his career when the accident was announced." He then continued in detective mode, pointing out a rather reasonable fact:
>
> "It's striking how much publicity

> Cinzano's death has garnered. Over there, a horse dies, and no one cares. When the mayor dies, they put out a notice. But in this case, there was an overwhelming amount of information when he died."

If true, the above would have raised suspicion, as no one would be interested in the death of a Uruguayan thoroughbred that had never raced in the United States. However, after searching the digital archives of American newspapers from back then, I couldn't find anything to support those claims. Perhaps he was referring to the notification sent to Uruguay via news agencies, and, if that is the case, we give him credit. He still had time for one more nugget: "I believe they won't be able to uncover anything over there because, if they dig too deep, they'll end up killing the winning horse as well."

We're already absolving the journalist and the winning horse of any suspicion. The article continues, and Forné seems to tone it down, suggesting that the switch could have been an unintentional error: "It's also true that if you send two horses that are somewhat similar, and when they arrive you mistakenly identify Lebón as Cinzano, or vice versa, the bridle gets switched…" But he closes the interview with the same intensity as he started it: "…and then they immediately take out the cheap one that's no good so that everything disappears, leaving the other one."

Later, we will see that Lebón's death was an accident that complicated everything Mark Gerard had set up over the years. However, it was impossible for this to be known in Uruguay at that moment, so Forné expressed an opinion similar to what any of us might have said at the bar with friends, and that's understandable. I almost forgot—the title of the article was also quite striking: "The Maffia [sic] Would Kill Anyone Who Investigates." The newspaper *El País*, in one of its subsequent articles, was already starting to be wary of the information received initially about Cinzano's death:

> In our previous edition, we stated that although it was first announced that Cinzano had died in an accident involving the truck that transported him, rumors are now beginning to circulate that neither the horse's death nor such a truck accident ever happened. Instead, it is suggested that the horse in question, under an assumed name, is competing at a well-known racetrack in the United States, where he might have recently won, paying out a huge dividend in dollars.

The possible involvement of the mafia is mentioned again, as it was the most logical explanation the Uruguayan press could find early on. Upon hearing the news, no one could suspect that there was no mafia involved, and that the scammer was a respected individual of good standing who had also been Secretariat's veterinarian. The newspaper also denied that the horse was owned by Kojak; while the actor had a passion for racing, his stable was located in California, on the west coast, while the horse was racing in New York and New Jersey, on the east coast.

As the days went by and more information emerged, *El País* and *Mundocolor* were no longer filled with wild conjectures and theories; their investigation was becoming the foundation that would support and enhance future investigations by the American press, setting a high standard for their colleagues. On October 25, the Daily News published another article stating that the investigation carried out by the NYRA was progressing as it awaited mail from Uruguay. In this article, it was mentioned for the first time that Cinzano's owner had collected a $150,000 insurance payout, and it was also noted for the first time that the horse that had died on Gerard's farm had been cremated. The avalanche had begun, with no end in sight. That same day, with the journalistic information and the records from the Uruguayan Jockey Club in hand, the NYRA pressed the red button, which detonated the bomb: Lebón was not Lebón.

On Wednesday, October 26, the racing pages of American newspapers were focused on one thing: the ringer, the sting, '*el cambiazo*,' (Translator's note: Quite literally, the "switch.") as we call it in the Río de la Plata region. In a press conference organized by the NYRA, its chairman, Ogden "Dinny" Phipps, was quick to say that this was the first case of fraud at a New York racetrack in the last thirty years. The police had identified a bettor who had wagered $1,600 on Lebón and walked away with $87,000 in cash in a paper bag; the bets had been placed at different windows to avoid raising suspicion. Another association executive confirmed that both Mark Gerard and Jack Morgan were suspended from their duties and banned from racetracks during the investigation due to their unsatisfactory statements. In the same inquiry, Joseph Taub, Cinzano's owner, was cleared of any wrongdoing. The following day, the Daily News published an article in which William Barry (president of the New York State Racing and Wagering Board) mentioned that, according to information provided by Interpol, the horse that was not Lebón could be Cinzano, another Uruguayan horse imported on the same trip. He also suggested that Lebón might not even be the dead horse but that he could be frolicking in some pasture, oblivious to all the commotion surrounding his name. He reached this conclusion after questioning the person responsible for removing horse carcasses to turn them into dog food. The guy not only hadn't taken any bodies from Gerard's farm, but he also didn't even know what they were talking about. Barry stated, "I choose to believe," and later confirmed with another source that some dead horse had indeed been taken from Gerard's farm, but surely not around the time Cinzano and Lebón were there.

In two days, the Daily News went from saying that Lebón had been cremated on the farm to claiming he was alive because he hadn't become dog food. For me, the second hypothesis confirms the first, but I'm not one to go against animal welfare, so for a moment, I'll subscribe to Barry's theory: Lebón did not die on the farm. In the same edition, journalist Wes Gaffer questioned whether the race could have been avoided and criticized NYRA veterinarians, as one of those responsible for checking horses and records noticed that the 'star' on the horse's head did not match the one on paper. When consulted about this, Dr. Manuel Gilman (head veterinarian at NYRA) responded that the only way to stop a switcheroo is if the horses have a tattooed lip like in the United States; otherwise, there was nothing that could be done. At that time, there were three horse identification methods approved by the Jockey Club in the United States:

- The birth certificate, recording all the horse's birthmarks.
- The lip tattoo, preferred by the National Thoroughbred Racing Association and done for free on horses racing at their tracks.
- The universal horse identification system, which

based its accuracy on the nighteyes, the "calluses" that horses have on the inner side of their legs—each one unique, like human fingerprints.

While the tattoo system was used at most tracks in the United States to identify horses, the tracks in New York preferred the universal system. This system had been created and patented by the Pinkertons (Belmont Park's security employees were called Pinkertons because they belonged to the security company of the same name.) working there and consisted of photos of the "calluses," a profile photo, and a front-facing photo of the animal; all of this was added to the horse's file, which included its birthmarks. According to Manuel Gilman, they didn't disregard any system, but he stated: "…we identify *the horse*. We are concerned with God-made marks, not just looking at a number." I swear he said that—isn't it lovely, the impunity that over twenty-five years in the same job gives you! Gotta love Manuel. In the same interview, the head of the *Pinkertons*, Jeremy O'Grady, said that he didn't dismiss the tattoo system because it was a good complement: "I'm not knocking it. It's a quick way to identify horses. But the only positive identification is natural markings. A mark which a man makes on an animal can be duplicated on another animal." He had a point, although, according to Jockey Club authorities, it had only happened once in Kentucky, and they quickly caught the culprit.

Dr. Gilman described how the identification of the horses that run in New York for the first time works:

> Before a horse runs […], three identification groups have to be satisfied; the *Pinkertons*, the TRPB and our own identifiers. On the day of a race the horse is checked twice. A veterinarian examines him at the barn in the mornings, looking for distinctive physical markings and verifying the lip tattoo, if the horse has one. While the horse is being saddled an identification expert compares him to photos on the Universal System card and then, in the walking ring, notes his nighteyes.
>
> We take horse identification very seriously. Our system is very expensive, with a full-time staff of nine in addition to the photographers.

October 28 began to gain center stage in the story of Mark Gerard, the mastermind behind all this and the one responsible for your reading this book. In his first visit to the courthouse regarding this case, Gerard and his attorney claimed that an indeterminate sanction was illegal, since nobody can be suspended without a prior hearing to present their defense. These arguments aside, they did have a technicality in their favor: the suspension had come a few hours before the accusation, so they brought out the full repertoire white-collar criminals usually resort to: "Do you see how they tarnish my reputation?," "Owners and trainers are dismayed by these false accusations to my client." And the best one of all: "My bets on the horse were an act of innocence; otherwise, I would never have asked the guard to walk with me to the car after collecting the winnings." He was so sure he would get away with it that, with his eloquence, in this day and age, he could have started his own streaming channel after the trial.

While the veterinarian was using that angle to handle the penalty, outside the main scene, Jack Morgan was beginning to plan his next moves. Without the economic solvency of his boss, he could not allow himself to go down with that ship. Thus, along with his lawyer, he devised a defense that ran parallel to Gerard's, collaborating from the start with the New York authorities. The third accused was the horse, who, incredibly enough, was placed under preventive detention (?) by prosecutor Dillon (in charge of the federal insurance fraud investigation) in stall number 59 at Belmont Park. Well, perhaps it was not so unbelievable, they still weren't aware of the extent of the scam, and the horse was the key evidence in the insurance fraud case; if they sent him out of the racetrack, he would probably end up at the nearest slaughterhouse, so they moved him to the stables, well guarded by FBI agents, who were the office investigating the insurance fraud.

I previously mentioned that, on the day he won, some

guy who worked at Belmont Park had noticed that Lebón's marking was different from the one from the review; as it happens, on October 28, it also came to light that the identity certificate they submitted for the race at Meadowlands two weeks after the meet had been tampered with: there were no longer differences between the marking in his head and the one in the drawing. Not even a week into the investigation, and the "criminal organization" was already bursting at its seams. By the end of the month, and with all things related to Cinzano-Lebón well underway, the authorities began to look into some of Gerard's other imports, as he had been taking horses from the Rio de la Plata region up north for years. The switch that was uncovered after the investigation at hand was that of the Uruguayan As de Pique II and the Argentine Enchumao.

Both horses had been taken to the northern country in 1975 by Mark Gerard; the Uruguayan was sold to Joe Parisi for 55,000 dollars, and the Argentine remained in Gerard's stud to run under his wife's name. Both started their North American campaigns in 1976 and ended them in 1977. Enchumao had strong performances since his debut, earning over $145,000 in prize money, winning the Fort Lauderdale Handicap at Gulfstream Park, and even competing in group races, but without any luck. Sadly, he lost his life on the track on the afternoon of February 26 while running in the Gulfstream Handicap (Group 1). In contrast, Aurreko's son struggled in his early allowances and dropped in class to secure two wins in lucrative claimings. However, when the Cinzano-Lebón case broke, he was subjected to tests to determine his identity, which they were never able to confirm. According to Dr. Manuel Gilman, the horse known in the U.S. as As de Pique was actually Enchumao. He argued that the *modus operandi* with these horses was the same as with Chirico-Sundoro, Lebón-Cinzano, which I will explain as follows: Gerard purchases two similar-looking horses in South America, one with a superb campaign and the other with no notable achievements; he arrives in the United States and sells the good horse for an important figure, keeping the horse that appears to be slower. When they reach North American racetracks, the tables turn: the one who was a star in South America barely manages to win a claiming race, while, with Gerard, the one who was barely a handicap horse turns into a contender in allowances and stakes. Lebón's death was not premeditated, but an accident (which is the only thing that's real in Gerard's account); otherwise, the veterinarian and his wife would also have murdered Sundoro and Enchumao to collect the insurance of Chirico and As de Pique, respectively. To sum up, the winner of the Fort Lauderdale Handicap was Uruguayan, so let's celebrate.

On November 1st, news of the switch leave the racing pages for the first time, taking residence in the crime section—they even share the page with the trial of David

Berkowitz, the tragically infamous "Son of Sam," who murdered six people in cold blood and injured seven others. There is a fine documentary on Netflix that raises the hypothesis that Berkowitz didn't act alone, and I find it very well-argued. I don't know how it relates to this story, but I didn't want to miss the chance to recommend that series.

In statements gathered by the *Daily News*, the D.A. of Nassau County, Denis Dillon, reported that as from November 4, an investigation into the fraud case was to be conducted through a grand jury, which surprised experts due to the speed with which the entire judicial machinery had been set in motion. In light of this shocking development, the lawyers of the accused, led by Neil Shayle, kept insisting that there was no evidence, and that everything was based on rumors and speculation. However, they also began to adopt a defensive stance, as Gerard claimed that the fault lay with international horse racing and its rather dubious animal identification system.

The following day, another bucket of cold water would fall upon the Muttontown farm: it was officially confirmed that the identities of Argentine horses Chirico and Sundoro, also imported by Mark Gerard, had been swapped. Something that caught the eye of the investigators was that Sundoro was claimed on two occasions by Christa Mancuso, a friend of Gerard's, who had also owned Enchumao (As de Pique).

Meanwhile, the attorneys were working against the clock to delay the trial for the other charges that did not include the insurance fraud. In this case, they filed an objection against Judge Francis Altimari for having read confidential documents from the New York Racing Office investigation. The judge was removed from the case, and Gerard puffed up his chest again, repeating that Cinzano had died on his farm. With regards to that event, the authorities had the theory that the horse's skull had been dumped at a landfill on Long Island, where there were 60,000 tons of trash. As incredible as it may seem, they conducted a search at the site with the hopes of finding the remains; as funny as it may be, this actually happened. They didn't find anything useful for the case, of course—only two or three skeletons, none resembling Cinzano/Lebón.

The case had been on all newspapers for a week, so they had to fill in the gaps with garbage because the real news was running out as the investigation reached a plateau. The press needed the audience's attention, and what better way for people to take sides and start hating the defendant than by talking about the suspect through anonymous sources and unreliable quotation marks. On the same page where the events were discussed, an article appeared featuring information from "anonymous neighbors" who claimed they were "not at all surprised" by Gerard's news. They reported that trucks with horses frequently arrived at night and left the next morning. They also mentioned that the Gerard couple was very private and did not interact with others. With the exception of a young man, who claimed the veterinarian had had an argument with his father because his dog had bitten some equine accessories, and after that argument they had started getting obscene calls from Gerard himself. Now that 45 years have gone by, we can write about it and it's even funny, but it amazes me the lengths a journalist will go to fill a void and keep the news alive.

On November 3rd, the novelty was that the insurance company Lloyd's of London would also file a lawsuit against the beneficiaries of Cinzano's life insurance. This insurance was for $150,000, which was paid almost immediately. The insurance money was collected by Joseph Taub's company, which appeared as the horse's owner, but the center of attention was, evidently, Mark Gerard and his maneuver. In parallel, the NYRA and the Jockey Club were expanding the main investigation, having already surveyed ninety horses in suspicious conditions or displaying inconsistent performances that might hint at a scam similar to the one pulled off by the veterinarian (for example, a horse who had just lost by ten lengths on a given week, would go on to win by two lengths in the next against the same contenders and with four-figure payouts… But wait, that still happens in every racetrack around the world. Could it be that no one is underperforming, and instead, all the horses have been swapped?)

In the meantime, at the courthouse in Nassau County, they granted Gerard's attorneys' request to lift the suspension. Jack Morgan benefitted from this decision as well. The reason for this was that the sanctioned individuals did not have the opportunity of an appropriate hearing to present their defenses before the suspension. This action marked Neil Shayle's last appearance as head of the defense, as the following day the veterinarian hired the famed Francis Lee Bailey, who had represented Patricia Hearst a few years earlier and would later be part of O. J. Simpson's defense team. Beyond Lee Bailey's fame and recognition, it was common knowledge that if you hired the criminal lawyer who defended the Boston Strangler and a war criminal involved in the My Lai massacre, among other crown jewels, you were basically declaring yourself guilty and entrusting your soul to whatever magic the man could work in court. With the new lawyer came a statement from Gerard, consisting of five points:

1. The two horses were identified by me at JFK airport on June 4, one as Cinzano, the other as Lebón.

2. Since NYRA does not require tattoos on the lips of imported horses, I had no way of knowing if the original certificate that accompanied the two horses was genuine or false.

3. The horse I identified as Cinzano suffered an

accident on June 12, which caused him irreparable injuries, for which he had to be euthanized.

4. I removed the body as quickly as possible for obvious reasons, in particular for the health and safety of the other horses in the stable, but I did so after a second revision carried out by another veterinarian.

5. Irresponsible leaks from the New York State Racing and Wagering Board led to unfair and damaging public opinions, and people began forming their own judgments. I wonder if anyone is still interested in conducting a careful evaluation of the facts.

To think that nowadays, one might fix everything with 'my account was hacked' or 'I fell for fake news'—not all times past were better times.

Around that time, authorities also sent five investigators to Uruguay, led by Joseph Mayer from the New York State Racing and Wagering Board. Their specific tasks were to interview trainers, jockeys, stable hands, and owners of the horses in question, as well as specialized journalists; collect blood samples from Tudor Park and Lemmy, the sires of Cinzano and Lebón, respectively; consult with relevant authorities about the process for exporting thoroughbred racehorses (out of more than one thousand horses exported in the past five years, ninety-eight had gone to the United States); and interrogate Luis Donamarí, Gerard's usual intermediary in the Rio de la Plata and the facilitator of the sale of the two horses.

While the scandal shifted to Uruguay and it seemed that the Cinzano-Lebón saga couldn't get any stranger, the name Larry Adams, the jockey who had led the horse to victory, appeared in the police news. According to a Newsday report, in response to a neighbor's complaint, the police arrested him at his home at 5 a.m. on November 4th, along with another jockey (Con Errico), for the rape of a 45-year-old woman who was still being held captive with the assailants at the time of their arrest. The woman reported that Adams had punched her and drugged her, rendering her semi-conscious, and then the two of them proceeded to rape her. Since New York at that time was a bit of a free-for-all, they paid a $1,000 fine and were quickly released from the police station. Adams continued racing throughout the year as if nothing had happened, even having a 20% increase in mounts in 1978 compared to 1977, and finished his career in 1983. This means that having the label of "rapist" stuck to his back did not negatively impact his business. Luckily, things are different in 2024, and athletes who engage in such behaviors are condemned by the justice system, and society. And, indeed, my sarcasm detector just broke.

In the same page, and more closely related to our story, word had it that Jack Morgan had made a deal with the prosecution and would testify for the State in exchange for immunity. The "caretaker" insisted that he had nothing to do with the switch, that he didn't know about Cinzano until it was published it in the newspapers, and that seeing Dr. Gerard almost every morning attending to and monitoring Lebón's exercises was nothing suspicious. Just kidding, I just made up the last sentence.

Going back to what was going on in Uruguay: journalists had spoken to Báez and Gelsi, who ascertained that "In our country there must be more than a hundred witnesses who can guarantee that the horse is Cinzano." Here, no one had the slightest doubt about the matter, that much was clear. The trainer was happy that Cinzano was still alive and mentioned that around the time that the champion had been sold, a blonde woman had been asking around the studs for a horse to ride, but not for racing. The blonde (unknown until then) was accompanied by two alleged Argentinians who claimed to be her interpreters. And I say 'alleged' because, in the article, Gelsi made it clear that, to him, they were far from being from the neighboring country (it would later be confirmed that they were, after all, Argentinians, and veterinarians at that: one of them was Jorge Diehl, Gerard's intermediary in Argentina). The article mentions that Cinzano slept in the stall by the kitchen, which from time to time earned him an extra apple or two, or even a plate of ravioli, but in moderation; he was an athlete, after all.

Interviews with almost everyone in Cinzano's circle took about ten minutes. Both Báez (who insisted that it wasn't fair for this to happen to "such a wonderful horse") and Gelsi immediately recognized him among thirty photographs. The rider explained to the reporters:

> "Cinzano has many markings that Lebón doesn't," Báez said. There is, for example, a larger shine or elongated white spots between the eyes; Cinzano has an injury on the front left leg caused when he was a year old: he hit a broken fence; he has a splint bone on one leg; a longer tail, and a height of 162 cm at the withers, which makes him shorter than Lebón. Báez also raced Lebón and won twice. 'But he's an ordinary horse, not very good,' said the jockey."

To finish, he mentioned that he had last seen the horse four or five days before he flew to New York, as the deal had been made with the trainer/agent Luis Donamarí, who had taken the horse to his stable, and from there they had made the final preparations before the trip. If before we said that interviews between the authorities and Cinzano's circle took no more than ten minutes, with Donamarí, it took two hours and a half, and the caretaker insisted that "if there was a switch, it was done in North America." The focus was on the person who had "put together the package" sent to the United

States, the one who had handled the identity certificates and had direct contact with Mark Gerard, as he had been the veterinarian's representative in Argentina and Uruguay for either three or seven years (depending on the source). Statements by Donamarí to the New York Times did not help him much during this interrogation: "Gerard requested a horse going for about $7,000 or $8,000, and I found Lebón for him, they never told me it had to look like Cinzano." As a result of this, the questions around the case multiplied. The prosecutor's representative, John Markson, was also interested in knowing what the relationship between the two was like and, above all, what had happened during Gerard's supposed visit to Montevideo fifteen days earlier, when the NYRA had already sanctioned him for the Cinzano affair. Apparently, Donamarí called the veterinarian to offer him the Uruguayan mare Wilca, a defender of the Haras San Miguel stud, who was under the care of Aníbal Cardozo and, according to the Uruguayan broker, "was the best in South America at distances shorter than a mile." The visit was not registered under any hotel, since Dr. Gerard was staying in the Argentine capital, but the sources consulted by the investigators assured that it had been a one-day visit: a conversation, then lunch, in which Jorge Diehl also participated, and back to Buenos Aires. After this encounter, Luis Donamarí visited the stud owned by Aníbal Cardozo, Wilca's trainer, asked the usual things before purchasing a race horse, and confirmed that the lesion she had back then was nothing serious. The fact that he didn't take any pictures made the caretaker think that perhaps the sale thing was just a rumor.

But it was no rumor; Gerard was genuinely interested in Wilca, although immediately after Donamarí's visit to the stable, the Cinzano case exploded in the U.S. and the sale was put on hold, despite Aníbal Cardozo, in declarations to the *Daily News*, saying that he hoped it would come through so the folks at the stud could make a profit. Luckily for Aníbal, Wildemauwe and the entire circle, the sale did come through a short while after, although given the history with Cinzano, the identity analyses were not confirmed by the North American Jockey Club for six more months. "Referred by a friend," the buyers were the Thomas brothers from Silver Creek Farm in Ohio, and they certainly made the most of the recommendation: in 1978, they raced her fourteen times between May and December, achieving four wins, including two stakes races—the Lady Mannequin Handicap and the Barbara Ann Handicap—and two allowance races. In 1979, she ran seven times between January and July, and won the Imp Stakes and an allowance; she ended her campaign with a fourth-place finish while aiming for a repeat victory in the Lady Mannequin Handicap. As a broodmare, she stood out by producing Dr. Bizzare, a champion at two and three years old in Ohio, as well as With Gratitude, who was a stakes-placed runner and the dam of Flat Rock, a stakes winner in Canada with nearly $350,000 in prize earnings.

Did you enjoy that little sideline? I didn't even realize it as I was writing; if the editor is into horse racing, he'll let it slide, because there's nothing we like more than straying from the topic when talking about racehorses. If the editor doesn't approve, I guess I'll just fire him.

Once the visit to Montevideo was over, the Americans, among whom was the head veterinarian with the NYRA, Dr. Manuel Gilman, would go back home carrying blood samples from Annabel Lee (Cinzano's mother, who was the only one of the four parents who was still alive), blood samples from horses directly related to the two ones involved, and the export certificates, that had been stored in a vault at the Central Bank from the beginning of the investigation. Dr. Gilman took advantage of the geographic proximity to Buenos Aires to collect other blood samples that would serve to clear any doubts in the other identity swap cases being investigated. An unsigned article published in Newsday assures that New York authorities had invited Forné, Báez, Gelsi and Donamarí to the United States to give their statements, but that they had refused out of fear that the mafia would kill them. However, this was such a blatant lie, that in the book *El justiciero* by Miguel Aguirre Bayley, Walter Báez and his wife can be seen enjoying the winter sun in the Big Apple; even Roberto Forné himself had his son living in the United States and collaborating occasionally with the investigation. Still, they had to fill the pages with anything—they probably took the first article they read on the case in our country and based everything off of that.

While the five investigators were flying from Montevideo to JFK, one could begin to see the figure of Alice Gerard in the scam. The veterinarian's wife emerged as a seemingly minor character, and entrusted her defense to attorney Richard Reisch, who swore that "through her passport he would prove that she had not been in Uruguay in May looking for a horse similar to Cinzano," but that, nevertheless, "the passport would show that she was in Uruguay for a couple of days, but she didn't remember the exact date." Come on, Richard, quit defending her.

The most important state witness regarding Mrs. Gerard's presence in Maroñas, as I mentioned a few paragraphs ago, was none other than Pablo Gelsi himself, who had accompanied her while taking pictures of Cinzano from every possible angle. At the same time, Jorge Diehl would testify before the Associated Press that in May he had accompanied Mrs. Gerard to Maroñas to see Lebón and Cinzano, so Alicia was just as involved in the scam as her husband.

According to a news report by Paul Montgomery and published by *The New York Times* on November 9, 1977, it was Diehl himself who first recommended that Mark Gerard buy Chirico, and the one who found Sundoro in 1976, both horses now being investigated for identity fraud:

> Dr. Diehl was concerned about his connection to the export of Chirico and Sundoro.
>
> He said that Dr. Gerard first decided to buy Chirico, who had won three or four races and sums ascending to $18,000… He described the horse in the identity certificate as a reddish-brown horse with no white markings. As Chirico awaited a place in a cargo plane to the United States, Dr. Diehl was surprised by a phone call from Dr. Gerard, who told him that his wife wanted a riding horse and asked him to find a cheap thoroughbred, specifying that it should also be a reddish-brown horse with no white markings. "I thought it was a bit suspicious, because in quarter horse races here, they sometimes swap animals, and it always happens with those that have no markings," he said. However, he stated, he kept complying with the request and soon found Sundoro, a six-year-old bay horse with no markings that had barely won a conditional race. He said that Chirico's trainer had found another stud for Sundoro. Also, that an owner had asked for $700 for Sundoro, and he phoned Dr. Gerard with the offer. "I told him he was a bad horse, but cheap, and he told me to buy it," the veterinarian recalled. Subsequent negotiations with the rest of Sundoro's owners made the price go up to twice the original $700, stated Diehl, and he also confirmed that Sundoro was a better horse than

what people thought. "I thought, then, that there was no point in a switch, because the horses were of the same quality," he went on.

Dr. Diehl said that the difference in coat color and size—Sundoro was larger—should have been enough to tell them apart. Also, that Chirico had four hair whorls around his neck. "If you pay attention to the identity documents, you could never swap those horses—he said—. But it seems that folks in the US aren't very good at identifying horses."

"I don't know what went on in the United States—the veterinarian continued—. But I'm afraid there might be a problem, because I'm concerned for the reputation of the Argentine horses. This news report is the only way I found to wash away my stupidity, if Mike Gerard made me the useful idiot."

Dr. Diehl emphasized that most of his progress in his career lately have been due to his association with Dr. Gerard. "The worse he did to me was beat me in four ping-pong matches at his home," said the Argentine.

Rewinding to our chronological order, in New York, after a week with no updates, the news was faltering, and in an attempt to keep making headlines, they began comparing the Belmont sting to the Watergate case. Consequently, Ogden Mills Phipps stepped in, saying that it was ridiculous because the Watergate case was a cover-up, whereas in this situation, the NYRA and the Jockey Club had notified about the investigation an hour after receiving the complaint from Uruguay. He insisted that the State of New York was way ahead than the rest of the country in terms of racing integrity, and that this had been the first case of a swap in the area in thirty years. The first case discovered, I would say, since after the Belmont sting, they started tightening the controls and several cases from years back emerged; switches were not unusual in racing at that time and had their peak in previous decades. The most famous character in this *métier* was Peter «Paddy» Barrie, who in his time had been known as *the king of the ringers*, practicing the art of painting over the horses' coats. He was so skilled with the brush that the fastest horses always looked identical to the slow ones they were supposed to represent. Additionally, he had great patience, and one example is more than enough.

In 1931, two horses were being transported to the Havre de Grace racetrack in Maryland. One of them was called Aknahton, and was a speedy three-year-old with four white legs. The other was a two-year-old gelding named Shem, who had two white legs and rarely arrived before the ambulance. He stopped the truck by the road, lit the scene with a couple of lanterns and began mixing paints on one side and resins on the other. He painted two of Aknahton's white legs and added all the small details he needed so that he would resemble Shem. Afterward, he began brushing his tail while applying resin and finished the job with the teeth: drilled a couple of black spots Aknahton had and filled them with porcelain, then cut the gums slightly with a knife to simulate an imminent loss of "baby teeth." But the most important detail was missing—you might say, how did he simulate he was gelded? He did that in the holding stalls at the racetrack on October 3 rd , shortly before the race: placing an obscene amount of ice on his testicles, by the time it was time to head to the parade, the horse's equipment was as tucked away as any man who has experienced extreme cold can imagine. The race was dull, "Shem" cruised along until the jockey made him run and he won by several lengths.

Years later, US police would begin Paddy's deportation procedure, whose earnings by that time neared $6,000,000, thanks to his artistic flair for counterfeiting living beings.

To the delight of journalists, on November 8, after statements by the NYRA's top figure made it to the press, the FBI confirmed that two agents were present in Montevideo. The reporters, who were at the duty-free shop[4] at Carrasco waiting for their boarding call, retraced their steps and hurriedly booked a couple of nights at a hotel. The testimony that interested the agents the most was that of Luis Donamarí, but after giving a statement to the New York investigators, he had vanished from the city—he was nowhere to be found, neither at home nor at the stud farm. His last statements had been: "I don't want them to make my life harder over something that wasn't my fault. The newspapers are making a soap opera out of this and I don't want to talk anymore; I didn't gain anything from this switch, they did that in the States, and I had nothing to do with it." After that public appearance, he would seclude himself until the storm had passed.

The next day, the news was the summons of Mrs. Alice Gerard to testify before the grand jury of Nassau County on November 10. However, her lawyer attempted to postpone her appearance by a week, arguing that she was "too distressed" to testify at that time, and in the process, negotiate immunity in exchange for testimony that seemed valuable to the investigation. While that was going on in court, Mark Gerard was banned from the stalls at Belmont Park, where he had to tend to four hundred horses, in spite of the judge's order that had lifted his ban. According to the guard who was standing in is way, the papers allowing him in had not yet made it to the NYRA's president's office. This infuriated his attorney, Neil Shayne, who began threatening with contempt letters and other antics angry attorneys usually resort to. I don't know why, but I can also picture him doing the "hold me back, or I'll kill him" routine against the Pinkerton acting as the doorman.

---

4 Carrasco Airport, the main air terminal in Uruguay, which likely did not have a duty free shop at the time.

All that commotion at the entrance was expected to be replayed the next day, but that same Thursday afternoon, the Attorney General's Office sent an order preventing the lifting of Gerard's suspension, thereby nullifying the decision made the previous Wednesday. I don't understand any of this either, but the veterinarian was once again sanctioned, and, as a bonus, the trainer Jack Morgan was too. As if there weren't enough problems already, a warning was received from New Jersey and California that there could be an identity issue between two horses imported by… none other than Mark Gerard. One of them was the Argentine Mariolo, who had arrived in the United States in 1974 and had first been sold for $22,000 through the veterinarian. After three years without a win, the horse raised at Haras La Constancia had changed hands and was now wandering through the cheaper claiming races in Pennsylvania. The other was Boots Colonero, the undefeated horse who had travelled in the same shipment as Lebón and Cinzano in mid-1977 and had gone to the western part of the empire, to the stud farm owned by Daniel Agnew. At the time of the complaint, he had only run two races in North America, with one second place and one no performance in respective allowances. Mr. Agnew and his father conducted dozens of business transactions with Gerard, but by now, the veterinarian's reputation was in the gutter by his own doing. Therefore, he also ordered identity tests from the Jockey Club, all the while keeping the horse racing; "one thing is one thing, and another thing is another thing," as the great Alfredo would say.[5] In the end, the only irregularity that came to light with this horse was the aforementioned change of nationality, so that Boots Colonero ceased to be Panamanian, and went back to being an Argentine again.

One month after the call by Julián Pérez and Daniel Rodríguez Oteiza to the Jockey Club, a lot of things had happened. What had yet to occur was for the events to transcend the world of horseracing and the police reports. This finally happened on November 14, 1977, when the legendary Sports Illustrated dedicated its cover page and main article to the Belmont "sting".

The beginning of the article is well worth transcribing, since it is a series of bullet points summarizing what was known of the case up to the moment:

> Now listen very carefully. This is the story of two racehorses from Uruguay. One is among the best in the history of that nation; the other, a $600 piece of waste. It is the story of a vet who takes care of purebreds as illustrious as Secretariat, of an elegant blonde buying a horse in Montevideo, of a jockey not particularly known for his talents, who brings in a 57-1 longshot at Belmont Park, of late-night training sessions, of a dead horse found in a city dumpster, of a $10,000 bet that went wrong, and a $1,300 bet that went right. It's the case of a switcheroo at the most famous racetrack in the United States, and a

$150,000 insurance fraud.

There's nothing missing, except mentioning the FBI to make the story more interesting, but that's my problem; ultimately, the FBI was only investigating the insurance fraud, which is the least interesting thing of all. The article mentions that cases like these happened regularly in less serious racetracks, such as those in Florida, but never in the birthplace of horse racing aristocracy (hence the refrain of the "first case in thirty years" that Ogden Phipps repeated ad nauseam).

The review highlights the $1,300 to win and $600 to place that Gerard bet at various windows in the racetrack, the $80,440 he collected thanks to the 57-1 payout, and mentions an incredible rumor (false, in light of the facts) that the Uruguayan journalists didn't find out about the switch until received a call from a mysterious blonde who had wagered $10,000 on Lebón's first race without being warned that he was going to throw the race and that the scam would occur in his second outing. Oh! What would become of 20th century police stories without female resentment?

The testimony of Pete Lombardo, a bureaucrat related to the insurance payment, also appears, admitting to having blindly trusted the death certificate sent by Mark Gerard and Harry Hemphill: "'After all, they take the Hippocratic oath or

---

5 *Chamarrita de los milicos*, Alfredo Zitarrosa, 1970.

something like that. Besides, how could I suspect Secretariat's veterinarian?" Trusting can go wrong, Pete.

Cover of the November 14, 1977 edition of *Sports Illustrated.*

The jockeys interviewed by Sports Illustrated preferred to remain anonymous, but they said that sometimes it seemed as if the South American horses imported by Gerard would run under other names and radically change their performance on the track. On the other hand, a client and friend of the veterinarian's, by the name Jack Price, could not believe what had been uncovered with this case: "It has to be some Dr. Jekyll and Mr. Hyde kind of thing, nothing makes sense here. Why risk a switcheroo if he can make $250,000 a year just by giving phenylbutazone injections?"

Although they acknowledge they are unclear as to whether Jack Morgan took part in the arrangement, they hint that he had some suspicion about Lebón's age, as he unsuccessfully tried to have another veterinarian examine his teeth, and they return to Morgan's offer to undergo a lie detector test to confirm his innocence.

The rumor that Lebón never died has some additional evidence to support it, as the transporter Anthony Mineri is mentioned as responsible for picking up a dead horse in Muttontown and then take it to the Huntington landfill. However, upon examining the skeleton found in that landfill, that presented a cranial fracture, it was confirmed to be a seven year-old animal, not a four year-old like Cinzano or five year-old like Lebón. The journalist closes the article by discussing the genuine concern of horseracing enthusiasts about the horses that enter the United States, "Now one could import a mule as a thoroughbred and it would go unnoticed," he rightfully says, but Jockey Club authorities at the time, as they devised a new system for animal control, hid behind the honorable nature of individuals and the naive belief that "honorable men do honorable things; most people involved in horse racing are honest".

November gone by, both the NYRA and the Nassau County District Attorney's Office had enough information to take Mark Gerard to court—only his statement and that of his wife before Prosecutor Dillon were missing. The entities in charge of both processes had statements from witnesses and transcripts of the interviews carried out in Uruguay, aside from a sworn statement by Dr. Manuel Gilman, in which he claimed that not only Cinzano/Lebón had been switched, but that, after having seen the photographic evidence in his visit to the Río de la Plata, their track records in their countries of origin and their performance in U.S. tracks, he was convinced that Chirico/Sundoro and As de Pique/Enchumao had also been subject to identity switches. Mark Gerard's crimes, according to the State of New York, were several: obtaining a false registration for a racehorse, running a horse under a false name, racing a painted horse to conceal marks on its body, and having a trainer and an owner knowingly compete with a swapped horse. The NYRA added to all of this that its regulations prohibited a veterinarian from owning racehorses. The most bizarre document submitted in court so far, for me, was the statement from insurance agent John Weiss, who said he had only seen a picture of a broken horse leg and had taken

Gerard's account as valid. He was less eager to work than I was. He's such a hero, though.

At this time (so far), an anonymous testimony came to light claiming that, although Cinzano had been taken to Jack Morgan's stud farm in Belmont Park at the end of August, Mark Gerard had him training in Saratoga for over a month under the name of Denim. Before taking the horse to Morgan, the veterinarian had obtained a foreign registration certificate under the name of Lebón using photos of Cinzano, as claimed in the evidence collected by the NYRA. According to the trainer, when he got to the stud farm with the horse, he handed over the registration certificate and a fake sale invoice. Since Morgan had been Gerard's assistant and had obtained his caretaker license thanks to the star veterinarian, he accepted doing this favor for him without ever suspecting what lay behind it. Gerard gave him $5,600 for the horse's maintenance and clarified that all proceeds would go to him, minus 10% corresponding to the trainer; an arrangement similar to the one he had with another horse called Blithe Reward. The statement also included the anecdote from when Gerard decided to register the horse in the claiming race for $10,000 that would be run on September 9. In his role as trainer, Morgan questioned the decision, since Lebón had had less than ten days to prepare, to which Gerard replied: "This is my call, not yours." It was crystal clear who the legal owner was and who called the shots.

On Monday, December 5, the veterinarian was scheduled to appear before the Nassau County court, since on Friday afternoon, the grand jury had decided to continue with the accusation upon seeing the evidence previously described as well as many other pieces of evidence. Mrs. Alice Gerard was summoned for Friday, December 9, but she had yet to negotiate an immunity agreement, which made her presence before the court uncertain.

Gerard's hearing was completely detrimental to his interests since, after hearing his testimony, the grand jury decided to accuse him of three felonies and six misdemeanors. Gerard himself surrendered to Judge Henderson at three in the afternoon. The once-respected professional now faced the following charges: second-degree grand larceny, falsification of business records, two counts of manipulating a sporting contest, one count of filing a false insurance claim, one count of witness tampering, and two counts of fraudulent practices in speed competitions. The two counts of second-degree grand larceny were related to the theft of Cinzano from Joseph Taub and the insurance fraud against Lloyd's of London and its subsidiary in the United States. The charge of falsification of business records pertained to the inducement of Dr. Harry Hemphill to sign an emergency visit to Muttontown in his activity log on June 12, the date on which Cinzano allegedly died. This signature allowed Gerard to conceal the theft of the horse from Mr. Taub. The witness tampering charge also tied him to Dr. Hemphill, as he had made him sign and certify blindly what he had told him. What were the penalties if everything went wrong? Seven years for theft and fraud, four years for falsifying records, and one year for the other misdemeanors. If he wanted to await trial at home, he had to pay a $100,000 bail, approximately 65% of what he had earned with Cinzano from the sale to Taub until the victory at Belmont—a veritable bargain.

The only one of the three who could face charges was Gerard; his wife (who was currently estranged) was awaiting a grant of immunity to testify, and Jack Morgan was already a prosecution witness. On the surface, it seemed that his wife had left him to fend for himself, but we will later see that this was not the case; it was all part of her defensive strategy. What seemed certain was that no strategy was going to save him from the losing streak he was going through. The following incident is just an example, as ridiculous as it was out of context: while they were taking him to be booked along with other criminals, the patrol car transporting them crashed into a car that didn't stop at a red light.

The preliminary hearing was set for January 4, 1978, so it wouldn't be a merry Christmas for the veterinarian, who, in addition, was being pointed out by prosecutor Dillon as responsible for another twenty-four switches at the three New York racetracks (Belmont Park, Saratoga, and Aqueduct).

Meanwhile, Jack Morgan was initiating a lawsuit against NYRA for a sum of $125,000. Both agreed to arrange for a self-suspension of their activities at New York racetracks. In Morgan's case, it was with the promise of having a hearing a week or ten days later to see if he could lift the penalty definitively because, according to his lawyer, he had violated a minor rule. In contrast, Gerard's lawyer's decision was to avoid a civil trial before the criminal trial, as another legal confrontation "would have completely affected the most important trial."

Morgan's hearing came two weeks later and only lasted ten minutes; what did take longer was the deliberation by the NYRA board, led by its president, William Barry, which lasted forty minutes. After the analysis, Barry himself stated that Morgan's suspension would remain in effect until December 31, 1977, but he could apply to regain his license starting January 1, 1978. Both the officials and Morgan's lawyer agreed that concealing the identity of an owner was not a crime, so he would have the opportunity to return to his work if he met all the requirements. Amidst all this chaos, Morgan had lost the few owners he had, with only David Soblick, a friend from South Carolina, willing to support him, who planned to send him six more horses for the stable, which was now managed by his father. The sanction had been imposed on October 24, so by the time the board made its decision, he had been away from his duties for 55 days and would reach 66 before obtaining a new permit. Since October 24, Cinzano had also been detained without bail, now occupying 'pavilion' 59 of 'the jail' at Belmont Park.

January arrived, along with the preliminary hearings and the testimony of Walter Báez. The Uruguayan jockey had traveled to identify Cinzano at the request of the prosecution—his arrival was film-worthy. Upon landing at JFK, they had him exit through a special area, surrounded by FBI agents; although the fear of the mafia being involved had dissipated, the entire operation did nothing but increase the anxiety that the Uruguayan felt, who was traveling with his wife.

> We got out of the airport and were ushered into an armored car. The caravan was comprised by four vehicles: two in front and one behind, ours being the second to last. The entire time, the agents talked to each other on walkie-talkies as I tried to figure out what was going on, making gestures as if I were Bernardo, the Zorro's sidekick. We finally got to a rather isolated motel, where we were kept under guard until it was time to testify. It wasn't a quick affair because we arrived in the middle of winter, and a snowstorm delayed everything. In total, we spent 25 days in New York, and what really left a mark was that after a year without

seeing him, the horse recognized me. I started calling him by his nickname first and then by his name: "Negro! Negro! Cinzano!"... at that moment, he reared up, started whinnying, and approached me. I was trembling with emotion. They asked if I wanted to ride him, and I said yes. We took a walk inside the facility where he was 'detained,' flanked by heavily armed FBI agents. It was an unforgettable experience.

Báez's statements to the American press were recorded in an article by *El País:*

> It is indeed Cinzano. I have no doubt about it. I saw the horse for two days in a row and the last time, I rode him and we went for a walk.
>
> They showed me many horses. Four or five horses that looked alike, with the same hair and the same height, but I recognized him right away. From the first moment, I knew which one Cinzano was.
>
> He is 25 kilos heavier than when he was here. He is very fat. They do keep him under permanent surveillance. They don't leave him alone for one second.
>
> I did not testify before the judge. I went with the members of the investigative group to see the horse and told them which one it was. I also did not sign any statement.

> The horse, from what I heard, will remain in the United States until the trial is over. Then, he will not be allowed to race or go inside a stud farm. That's all I know about Cinzano's future.

Báez's contribution, plus other evidence and the thirty-eight witnesses presented during the preliminary hearing led to the confirmation, on February 10, of the previously presented charges and, also, two new charges: attempted bribery of a witness and witness tampering. The first charge was related to his offering money to his friend Christa Mancuso to falsify her testimony before the grand jury. Did Mrs. Mancuso refuse the cash and turn him in? Never. Investigators discovered that Gerard had sent her $1,000 before she testified. For this charge, he faced up to seven years in prison. The other charge was a misdemeanor and involved the trainer Joseph McMahon from Saratoga, the anonymous figure who testified that Gerard had brought Cinzano, under the name Denim, to train at that racetrack before taking him to Jack Morgan.

It seems that good ol' Mark wanted to tell him it was not quite like that, that he shouldn't say that, that it wouldn't do any good, etc. The prosecution found out, and boom, another charge. Luckily, this one only carried a maximum sentence of one year. He dodged prosecution because the lawyer played the "My client is ill" card, given that, in addition to his admission to Lake Worth Hospital for heart failure on January 23, Gerard spent all of February alternating between the hospital and his home. On February 24, his attorneys reported that he had once again been hospitalized due to a heart attack and that, at the request of his doctors, they did not recommend he did any traveling or strong emotions, and that they should postpone Gerard's appearance in court until March 27. Well, the travel thing was not exactly like that, since he was based in Miami while recovering, but if you have F. Lee Bailey as your attorney, you can pretty much do whatever you like. On March 27, he finally traveled to New York to plead guilty of the new bribery and witness tampering charges. So much fuss for something as predictable as *Despacito*;[6] bureaucracy: 1 – common sense: 0.

His wife, Alice, was not doing any better. After declaring before the grand jury on February 17, in a hearing lasting several hours, she was summoned again to continue her testimony on February 21. But after leaving the courthouse, she admitted herself to Gracie Square Hospital in Manhattan, citing a depressive episode, which postponed the continuation of the testimony until March 6. Mrs. Gerard remained at that center for one week and then transferred to the Silver Hill Foundation,

---

6 *Despacito*: A massively popular Latin pop song, widely played during the southern summer of 2018. The original version, by Luis Fonsi, was released in January 2017.

a psychiatric center located in Connecticut, which meant she was still unable to declare on the new scheduled date. Her attorney, Stephen Peskin, came to court with a telegram sent from said establishment, in which they assured that Alice Gerard had voluntarily come in on March 3 with a clinical picture of severe depression and was being subjected to drug treatment, needing permanent surveillance, and her presence in court was strongly discouraged. With this notification, Peskin made sure his client would not be charged with contempt.

There are several side stories in this case. I will now describe how the owners of Chirico, Sundoro, and As de Pique—the horses that became entangled in the investigation by coincidence and remained sanctioned—were faring.

Joseph Rapisarda was the owner of Sundoro. He had bought it from Christa Mancuso on May 16, 1977 after winning a race at Acqueduct; for this, he had to pay the $5,000 that the claiming demanded. On May 31, he won a claiming race at Belmont Park, afterwards came in fourth, also at Belmont, won in Atlantic City on July 2, and finished third in a handicap race in Delaware on July 24. After that streak, he went nearly three months without competing, until he was finally registered in Belmont Park on October 17. Since the Lebón case had come to light three days prior and all of the horses imported by Gerard were under suspicion, racetrack authorities demanded that he be removed from the race. "I'm a simple spectator in all of this—Rapisarda said—, if the horses are going to be sanctioned for life by NYRA, I propose that the entity purchase the animals from us for the price of the last claiming they raced, and then send them off to a farm. It would be a good business move."

"This guy is nuts", one of NYRA's top figures, James Heffernan, must have thought. But, since that can't be said out loud, he stated that "although they had had conversations with the implicated parties, they never even considered taking that proposal seriously." After seeing the investigators' pictures, Rapisarda confirmed that his horse was actually Chirico, but that in his stud farm was the horse he had claimed; no switch had been done. By that time, he had already sent the animal to a farm that charged him $8 per day against the $32 per day it would cost him to be in a stable; "I was told that I had to wait for things to get sorted out, but it seems nothing is getting sorted out here."

"This is unfair, it doesn't make any sense", Vincent Giorgis told the journalist Ed Comerford. Giorgis was the owner, along with his mother, of Bellrose Farm. Aside from Chirico, they had other six horses in training; just like Cinzano, his horse was also detained at Belmont Park, constantly surveilled by the Pinkertons. Unlike Rapisarda, he did not believe his horse to be any other horse; they had bought him on July 30, 1977, after coming in third place in a claiming race, for $5,000, but the animal had changed hands quite a few times. With the Giorgis, he had run in four races and had one victory on October 5, 1977, in a claiming race at Belmont Park. After that race, what we already know: investigation, detention and suspension. He was convinced that the NYRA ought to take responsibility for the horses and buy them, since, due to their shortcomings in terms of controls, they had been responsible for this situation. Giorgis filed a lawsuit against Rapisarda for damages because of the switch, but the lawsuit was dismissed. On November 18, 1978, the NYRA confirmed the definitive ban for both animals.

For Joe Parisi, the situation was different, since he had purchased As de Pique directly from Gerard for $55,000 and appeared to be "a victim of the circumstances". He didn't want to make any statements regarding the horse's identity, since that matter was being handled by his attorneys, but it was clear there was something fishy, because the horse had only achieved two victories in cheap claiming races, whereas his South American campaign had been exceptional. The horse was kept at a stall in New Jersey, but not under custody as the other horses involved; the NYRA had rejected Parisi's proposal to transfer him to Belmont Park, where he also had stalls.

The three were heartbroken, but the passion they felt for horse racing was stronger, and they never thought about giving it up. Giorgi also sued the NYRA for damages, with the hopes of collecting $16,000, since he accused them of negligence, but was dismissed.

Because of their lifetime suspension, none of the animals ever raced again after 1977. This sanction corresponded to the violation of Jockey Club Rule 59:

> No horse shall be entered or allowed to participate if the official regulatory body with jurisdiction over the infraction has determined that the person who had legal custody or control of the animal at that time knowingly entered or raced it under a different name than its own. Whether it was entered or raced.

As we will see further ahead, with As de Pique (Enchumao), they tried to run four years later in Meadowlands (New Jersey), but was vetoed by that State's organization.

Other main characters who had almost gone almost unnoticed among all the comings and goings were Joseph Taub and the insurance company Lloyd's of London, who, according to prosecutor Dillon, had to decide who would keep the horse. On March 28, five months after Cinzano was detained, the prosecutor resolved that, after the examinations conducted on the animal by the defense, the horse could return to its owner. But it wasn't that simple, there were a few caveats: first and foremost, the horse was dead. Second, if it was confirmed that it was confirmed that it was Cinzano and he was alive, did it have to go back to Joseph Taub or the insurance company, which had paid the policy amount? Third and last, neither of the two parties wanted to keep a race horse that was never going to race again. “Exhibit A,” as Cinzano was known, was going to be delivered to its owners in mid-April, but there were no owners to whom deliver it to. There was also the issue of money: who would take care of the $7,000 Jack Morgan had already spent on its upkeep? Taub’s attorney clearly said that his client had purchased Cinzano by Gerard’s recommendation, he never saw the animal, and, when he was informed of his death, he collected the insurance money, end of story. The Nets owner had had no part whatsoever in the scandal and was willing to give up the horse once it was out of custody. The outlook was no different at Lloyd’s: their attorney let them know that they “insured race horses, but had no intention of getting in the business of horseracing.” If it was legally confirmed that the horse was Cinzano, their only concern was knowing who would return the policy money, and little more.

On April 11, the defense carried out the revision of Cinzano. The horse was still in stall number 59, under the custody of Jack Morgan. The presence of the expert sent by the firm of F. Lee Bailey was only to create smoke and mirrors, since he was not a horse specialist or anything resembling one. The actual horse specialist was Barry Morgan—Jack’s father had extensive experience in caring for purebreds and now collaborated with his son at the stalls in Belmont Park. Barry would warn those performing the examinations that “he was a very strong and very tough horse,” and that if they were careless for just one second, “he could easily hurt them.” On the day prior to this instance, Warren Mainella, Jack Morgan’s attorney, He presented an order to cancel the delivery of the horse to Taub or Lloyd’s London, according to what prosecutor Dillon had decided. The arguments were understandable: The Morgans had financially supported the horse since it was confiscated and didn’t think it was fair that it would slip out of their hands without recovering the $7,000 they had invested up to that point. “This has me feeling miserable, they all promised me they would cover the horse’s expenses, but no one has paid me anything. My parents have put in money to feed the horse, but they are not in a position to take on the expense,” Jack Morgan told *Newsday* with a sadness he could not conceal. Maybe nowadays it is more usual for parents to take care of their thirty-two year old child, but in the 20th century, people that age were already self-sufficient adults, which explains the situation that Jack felt with regards to this situation. In addition, he was so fed up with the topic, that he made the pondered: “With all of the stupid things that have happened in this case, I wouldn’t be surprised if the horse was actually Lebón.” Hey, Jack, time traveler here—no, it was not, so quit getting your hopes up.

His attorney, Warren Mainella, was confident in the approval of the order that would grant the Morgans the authority to take the horse to a public auction, as he did not foresee anyone returning the money to the family.

THE TRIAL

The pretrial hearing was scheduled for June 2, and Gerard was trying to delay it by all means. On May 17, his attorneys submitted a motion to the Supreme Court of Appeals to change the venue of the trial since, according to the thirty news articles they presented as evidence, the local residents, including some members of the jury, had already made up their minds, making it unlikely that he would receive a fair trial. As this motion gained traction, the defense had succeeded in negotiating the bail, which was now set at $50,000. The argument for lowering the amount was that this entire incident had set Dr. Gerard back financially, and he had no way of facing the previous payment. He had even had to sell the Muttontown farm to pay for his defense—so moving. Perhaps if he had considered the consequences before making a living out of rigging races, none of this would have happened. Anyway, the judges know more than I do, so I guess they must have been right in lowering the bail amount.

On the day of the preliminary hearing, the press was focused on whether the defense would uncover the strategy to be used during the trial set to begin on September 6, or if they would take a passive stance at this stage. Defense attorney James Megberg, acting as F. Lee Bailey's representative in the pre-trial stages, went straight to the point. He requested the prosecution to provide the statement Alice Gerard had made to renowned criminal psychologist Daniel Schwartz, in which she admitted to having been involved in some of the horse swaps. This admission, in theory, would exonerate her husband from blame. The prosecution denied access to the full statement, arguing that it had been made while she was under psychiatric treatment. Releasing this information to the public might expose personal issues, potentially causing further psychological harm to Mrs. Gerard. Prosecutor Davenport said of her: "She inspired so much compassion in us that we decided not to arrest her." After these statements, the decision was now in the hands of judge Harrington. Surely the testimony was lacking in terms of paperwork and Gerard's defense didn't mind Alice being dragged through the mud so that their client's sentence could be reduced. It is worth remembering that, according to statements, when the Lebón-Cinzano affair came to light, they had split up after nine years of marriage (which is not at all suspicious). At the hearing, Megberg, as well as accusing Alice of being the brains behind the change, doubted whether the prosecution would actually present the thirty-eight witnesses it claimed to have, and asserted that the opinions of their experts had been most likely bought. He suggested that when the trial came, none of them would be able to recognize whether the horse in custody was Cinzano or Lebón.

One week after the pretrial hearing, prosecutor Dillon

gave the order to move the horse from the stall where he had been in detention since October 24 to the North Shore farm, "to safeguard the evidence"—indeed, the same evidence he wanted to give away to a millionaire and a multi-million dollar company a mere two months before, because they had enough evidence to confirm the horse's identity.

The reason? He didn't want the Morgans selling the horse before the auction ultimately scheduled for July. Jack and his attorney wanted to charge $33,000 for expenses incurred during the investigation, but the NYRA would only give him a third of that. The offer wasn't trivial; behind it was the prosecutor, who hoped that Mainella and Morgan would take the case to trial to prove that the horse was indeed Cinzano and start the trial against Gerard with a 5-0 lead. If a court of law were to prove that the horse was indeed Cinzano, the veterinarian would run out of options and the prosecution would have an easy win. The prosecutor's office couldn't care less if that meant financially suffocating the Morgans.

The trainer did not want to part with the horse; he had grown really fond of him and also knew what the animal could give once he was back in shape. He would be present at the July 10 auction and offer his services to the new owner—the scandal had ruined his finances and he needed for new owners to trust him. But come to think of it, how does anyone auction off a horse with an unknown name that would probably never be allowed to race again? Doing so without a name, as if it weren't a race horse, but an anonymous Belmont Park squatter, something disrespectful for a champion, but fitting his condition as inmate. Because as much as the prosecution insisted that the horse was evidence, to all intents and purposes, he was being treated as a convict. It was probably the only way of keeping the horse safe from any other move. But the fact of the matter was, he was the only one out of all those implicated, who was actually imprisoned.

One month after Gerard's attorneys requested the transfer of the trial to another courthouse, the Supreme Court of Appeals denied the request; the trial would still be held at Nassau County. By the way, prosecutor Dillon was told to quit messing around with the horse and not get in the way of the July 10 auction: the horse *had* to be sold no matter what, because the Morgans were up to their necks in unpaid bills. A win for the underdogs, three cheers for Douglas Young, the judge who signed the order.

Some days before the auction, it became known that Cinzano's turn would be at around 1 p.m., and he could be seen and checked out at one of the stalls in building number 40. He would be put up for sale as: "Registered as Lebón, but allegedly named Cinzano." The new owner would acquire the horse's titles but not the horse itself; it would remain under legal jurisdiction until the trial against Mark Gerard concluded.

The Morgans were praying to every saint they could think of for someone to pay the $33,150 (and counting) they had spent keeping the horse in captivity.

The auction was near, and there were more journalists hanging on Cinzano's future that on the retirement of the champion Forego, who on that July 10, had finished fifth in the Suburban Handicap (Group 1), raced six days before. What I've written just now is no joke—Forego was in stall number 10 of the stud barn, and there weren't even half as many journalists as those waiting for Cinzano at stall 40. The crowd was pushing and trying to get as close as possible to the railing so they could get a glimpse of the most famous horse in the United States walking by. The auctioneer didn't share the enthusiasm of the onlookers; he even seemed embarrassed about the task he was about to perform. Before the auction began, Warren Mainella clarified to those present that only the horse's ownership documents would be auctioned; the animal would immediately return to the farm in North Shore, with the District Attorney's office covering its maintenance until the end of the trial against Mark Gerard. Once the verdict was read, the horse would go to the highest bidder that afternoon.

"Is anyone actually interested in this horse?" asked Sheldon Weisser, the auctioneer in charge of the most famous sale of the decade, in disbelief. "If anyone at the back raised their hand, I couldn't see that, so if you could please put your hand up again". Not a fly was stirring. "I counted forty-seven people, but no hands raised" was the last thing he said before pausing the (non-existing) bid, to remind those interested that the one up for auction was a horse named Lebón, and that it was accused of being Cinzano, that the money collected would reimburse the Morgan family, that they were full of moths, due to these nine months of inactivity to which the horse had been subjected. Since the crowd seemed like a statue convention, he began to play his part and point out to nonexistent clients, hoping that someone would take the bait:

> I have 5000 for the horse, who gives more? I saw 6000 over there. Does anyone want 7000? Who said 7000? Very well, I have 7000 and now 8000. More than 8000? I'm sure there is, I have 8000, I have 9000.
>
> Any more offers? The gentleman said 10,000, anyone surpass the 10,000? Look, it's almost gone... 10,000 once, 10,000 twice, 10,000 three times!
>
> Sold to Mr. Jack Morgan.

Wait, what happened here? What do you mean, sold to Mr. Jack Morgan? *The* Jack Morgan, the one we've been talking about forever here? Yes, that Jack Morgan. Believe it or not, there was nothing fishy here. Granted, it is weird for a guy to buy his own horse at an auction organized at his stud, where after purchasing it, the buyer would have to send the horse to a farm, but there was a clause that roughly stated the following: “If the offer for the horse does not exceed the $33,000 that the Morgan family has spent on maintenance and training for the horse for the past nine months, Mr. Jack Morgan can make an offer and keep the animal.”

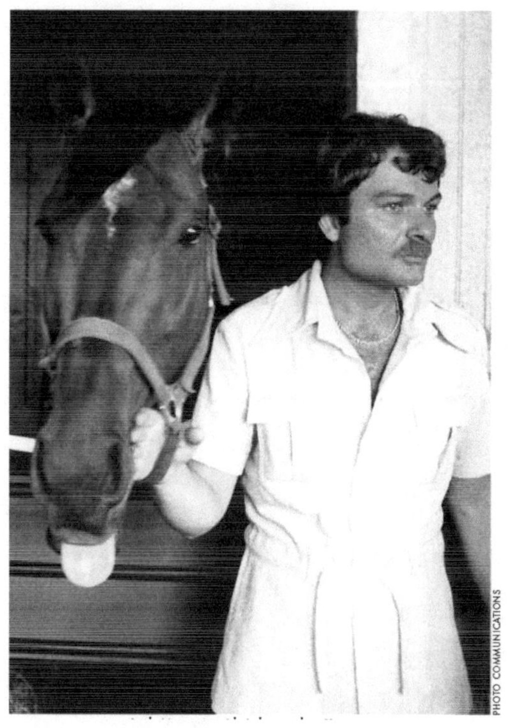

Cinzano and Jack Morgan. Photo: Ringers and Rascals, David Ashforth, published on Amazon in 2003.

The trainer was happy with the titles in hand, but the fight was not over. He had to wait until after the trial to bring the horse to his boxes and for the district attorney’s office to pay him the amount he wanted for these nine months of confinement. As if that weren’t enough, after the trial, he would have to fight to get the NYRA and the New York

Racing and Wagering Board to give the horse a chance to race officially again, despite the sanction that came with violating Rule 59. Additionally, he would also have to reaffirm his ownership of the horse since, when it went to auction at his request, the animal was still owned by Mark Gerard. He had stated that he was only the owner on paper, not in reality. Jack was in for a busy year, but we must know that he took a gamble on the horse because he saw potential—it wasn't just because he was a good guy.

The first good news since the start of this soap came for Mark Gerard on July 27: Judge Raymond Harrington confirmed the dismissal of five of the eleven charges against the veterinarian, so now the trial would be 'only' for six crimes. The charges that were dismissed were: bribery of a witness, the two charges involving witness tampering, and the two related to manipulating sports competitions.

According to the Judge, the bribery charge was dismissed because, although there was evidence that Christa Mancuso had received $1,000 before testifying before the grand jury, there was no evidence to support that the payment was made to alter her testimony. The witness tampering charges were dismissed because there was no evidence to confirm that Mark Gerard knew what Dr. Hemphill and Mr. McMahon would testify before the grand jury, and the minor charges of sports tampering were dismissed because, although

Gerard "presented a horse under a changed name, he did not fix the race to win it; he cheated, but did not manipulate the results."

With little more than twenty days to the trial, the U.S. Jockey Club introduced new methods for identifying imported horses; all of this due to the Lebón case. The first modification was that, upon confirming the import, the Jockey Club would contact its foreign counterpart to review the identity certificates before the animal left its country of origin. Until the arrival of Lebón and Cinzano, the importer was responsible for certifying the horse's identity. In this case, Gerard was the one who forged the identity certificates; he himself legitimized them upon his arrival at the airport, and he was the one who sent them to the Jockey Club.

An additional change was related to photographs: they had to be taken from specific angles and by a professional photographer. According to the head of the identification department at the Jockey Club, they often received laughable pictures "that seemed to be taken by a fourteen-year-old using a disposable Kodak camera."

The remaining adjustments were meant for horses born in the United States and Mexico, and continued to highlight the state of New York as the organization with the best photo identification method for the chestnut or night eye —the callosity present in horses' legs. They are all unique, much in the same way as fingerprints are to humans. But why wasn't this identification method used in the Lebón case? We don't know, and neither do they; they say that the error was carrying over from before, that the NYRA was never able to do anything about it.

A week before the start of the trial, when nothing else should have happened, Jack Morgan appeared in court requesting a judicial order allowing him to race Cinzano. The court set a hearing between NYRA, the Jockey Club, and Jack Morgan for September 6, the same date the State vs. Gerard trial was scheduled to begin.

On Wednesday, September 6, the courthouse was teeming with people. All those reporters following Cinzano's case (also referred to by the American press as The Dead Ringer, Caper, The Belmont Sting, The Switch), added to the regular court reporters, as the start of the trial was finally upon them. Despite being in the spotlight for almost a year, no one could believe that Mark Gerard was the main person responsible for this fraud. He was the single most respected veterinarian in the United States; until the scandal broke, he was attending to four hundred horses and had an impressive résumé that included Cañonero II, Kelso, Hoist the Flag, Riva Ridge, and Secretariat. Why did he need to ruin his reputation by changing the identity of so many horses? Maybe he was certain that, thanks to his contacts, he could make a seamless leap from horseracing to polo; maybe he enjoyed the money more than he enjoyed having a meal on his plate; maybe he needed the extra rush of adrenaline. We will never know for sure, but since the day "Lebón" entered the winner's circle at Belmont Park, his life had been in a downward spiral, and this trial could hasten his fall —unless, that is, F. Lee Bailey could work his magic and minimize the damage.

The trial had a slow start, since throughout the entire morning both parties were at Judge Harrington's office as the fifty spectators eagerly waited for some action in the courtroom. It wasn't until the afternoon that there finally was some, with the defense acknowledging a switch for the first time ever, but that the person responsible for it would have been Alice Gerard, and not her husband. They clung to the statements she had given prosecutors while she had been hospitalized for her psychiatric issues, but at the same time hesitated to put her on the stand due to her instability. Alice was living in California at the time of the trial, and Davenport, the assistant prosecutor handling the case, was aware that putting someone on the stand who had been in treatment for ten years might not be ideal. This September 6 also marked Lee Bailey's return to the courtroom since the Patricia Hearst trial, in which he had admitted to not doing a good job.

The prosecution was the first to select jurors, dismissing only one of the initial eleven because he was a racing enthusiast with a previously formed opinion. Davenport's key question to all potential jurors was: "Are you able to vote against Gerard even if you find the switch story amusing?" He feared that the bizarre details of the case—resembling a poorly written Venezuelan soap opera—combined with Gerard's charisma and the audacity and verbosity of the defense attorney, might evoke sympathy for the accused and overshadow the evidence. Lee Bailey, the defense attorney, posed a question aligned with this concern: "Do you think someone who hires me does so because they're guilty?" Embracing his notorious reputation, he prompted one prospective juror to reply: "If they're hiring the best lawyer, it's because they need him." That juror was the only one dismissed by the defense, leaving only nine jurors. To reach the legal number of jurors, they continued interviewing several prospects. Both sides questioned the candidates, leading to a surreal exchange where one was dismissed by the prosecution and another by the defense. The dialogue highlighted the peculiar dynamics of the case:

—Are you with the Animal Protection Society?

—Yes.

— Does it disgust you to see someone mistreating an animal??

—Yes.

—Do you think it is a heinous act?

—Well, remember the scene from *The Godfather*, that was awful.

According to the press, there were already one hundred people in the room by the second day (if the audience kept growing, they would need to read the verdict at Madison Square Garden), attentively following the counterpoint between the prosecutor and the defense attorney, which was oddly entertaining for the display of boredom trials usually are.

On Friday, September 8, the defense began to pound on Alice Gerard's responsibility in the switch, with the theory that the wife was the one responsible, the motive being taking revenge on the NYRA and the entire horse racing environment. According to Bailey, Mrs. Gerard "loved horses and hated horse racing for the brutality it unleashed on the horses", hence the idea to race a switched horse, to humiliate the industry. She "only changed the reins and Lebón became Cinzano and Cinzano became Lebón," then the accident happened and Mark Gerard put the horse down that he thought was Cinzano. Alice's plan was to "wipe down the face of races with a brush. She wanted to write a book and show the world how easy it was too fool the entire horse racing world being nothing more than the sophisticated wife of a veterinarian. She went out looking for a horse that looked like Cinzano, to teach them a lesson on top of making some money." He finished the argument by saying that his client had everything, that he gained nothing by setting up a scam to win $80,000, the classic from political campaigns: ‘he's rich, he doesn't need to steal’. Reading it again, it seems more like an argument by Lionel Hutz than from the best defense attorney in America; maybe in court, with his eloquence and charisma, the jury found this hypothesis credible—I see it as nothing but a beautiful delusion.

Thomas Davenport’s speech was less theatrical, as he simply read the charges and described Gerard’s engineering in service of the scam, which was only discovered…

> …because, as fate would have it, two Uruguayans were there that rainy afternoon at Belmont Park, surprised to see Lebón make it to the winning line. Coming closer to congratulate their acquaintances, they instantly realized that the horse in question was Cinzano. Back to their country, they mentioned the event to two journalists, who requested the winner’s photo from the Associated Press, clearing up all doubts. It was practically a perfect scam that only failed because of the honor and patriotic pride of two South Americans.

On Monday, September 11, it was Jack Morgan’s turn, the former veterinary assistant turned trainer, frontman, owner, and now prosecution witness. The courtroom was as full as in previous days; in this regard, the journalists no longer estimated a number to avoid unnecessary exaggeration. Lebón’s trainer was one of the prosecutor’s headliners, and, now that the immunity agreement in return for a testimony was confirmed, he began with an overdose of honesty: “I let Gerard register the horse under my name in hopes that the partnership with him, a prominent thoroughbred veterinarian, would help me make a leap forward in my career as a trainer”. He did so knowing that he was trespassing a rule that did not allow veterinarians to own race horses, but, since it was a quite frequent practice, he couldn’t resist the ambition of making it to the front page. When it was turn for Lee Bailey’s questions, most revolved around how, in reality, Gerard had never shown much interest in the horse, and the atmosphere got a little heated. At times, it seemed more like a bar argument than a witness interrogation; even Judge Harrington had to intervene and tell Morgan to calm down and stop arguing with the lawyer. The defense tried to discredit the testimony, claiming it had been arranged with the prosecution to allow him to continue training racehorses, and that Alice Gerard was the main person responsible for the fraud. After two hours, Morgan left the stand with the promise to return the next day.

The first witness of the day had been John Weiss, the insurance company employee who, thanks to his first statement, had turned into the guy with the least desire to work in the entire world. He said he hadn’t been able to examine the remains of the dead horse because Gerard had quickly gotten rid of the corpse, that he had trusted the report that spoke of a skull and leg fracture, and that he had only received the picture of a broken leg. When Davenport asked whether that photo might be of any horse, the answer was yes, which set up the counterattack for the defense lawyer, who asked: "And did you ask for photos of the horse's head?" With much embarrassment, the answer was no. With the photograph of a broken leg, the guy authorized the insurance payment of $150,000; if he wasn't in on the fraud, we're talking about the most apathetic insurance broker in the entire state of New York.

A third witness testified that day, Dr. Thomas Gorman, a veterinarian who received a call from Gerard on the day of the accident saying that Cinzano had been badly injured and had to be euthanized. He also asked that he draft a report of the event. Dr. Gorman refused, since he had not been in the farm to confirm the facts, but he was able to corroborate the leg fracture the next day when (now, pay attention to this) Mark Gerard took the broken leg to Belmont Park, to show how severe the lesion had been. What was wrong with you, Mark? Were you insane, bro? Going around carrying a broken horse's leg with you? After all, the lady in the jury who mentioned the scene from *The Godfather* was not that wrong. He didn't have the body because he had dumped it at the Huntington Town landfill, as Gerard had informed him. Thank goodness. Now I believe Dr. Hemphill signed the death certificate so he would throw the leg in the trash once and for all. *Je suis* Hemphill. Being serious now, the most likely scenario is that Gerard showed him the picture of the broken leg, but I choose to stick to the literal wording of the Associated Press wire, which went this: "Gorman said he declined go to Gerard's Muttontown home that night, but the next day he saw him at Belmont Park race track and examined a severed part of a horse's leg."

The attorney won the second round between Morgan and Bailey. He won by points, that much is true, but he deserved the KO. The following sequence was the one that had the trainer stumble:

> "—Isn't it true that you once said: 'This is my horse and I can do whatever I want?'
>
> —Yes, I told the farmhand Peter Romanger, but it was a lie; I said it to protect Dr. Gerard's reputation.

From that point on, Bailey started bombing the witness's statement with the aim of making him lose credibility thanks to that alleged confession to the farmhand. Morgan, visibly upset, wouldn't stop repeating: "Everyone involved in this case lied to me." The prosecutor wasn't in a better mood after seeing how his witness had been treated, and before excusing him, he made a question/statement: "The only one we know who lied was you, you lied when you claimed to be the owner of the horse, but that wasn't true, right? You were the necessary person, you were the functional fool that every scam needs".

The day took a 180° turn when the prosecution

presented a recording of Mark Gerard's statement before the New York State Racing and Wagering Board on October 23, 1977. In the recording, the veterinarian could be heard saying that he could "without any doubt" tell the difference between the two horses. This undermined the defense's argument that the switch had been made without his knowledge:

> —There was never the slightest doubt in my mind, Lebón seemed to be a classless, mediocre horse, and Cinzano had the stature of a good horse, he looked bigger and better than the other one.
>
> —The horses were the same size, same color and same white markings in the forehead?
>
> —To a rookie, most likely so.

In light of this irrefutable evidence, Bailey told the press that he had not yet decided whether Gerard would take the stand to give his version of the events to the jury.

September 13 was the day when journalist Julián Pérez testified. He had traveled specifically to New York to give his testimony and ended up closing the court session. He said that he knew Cinzano and Lebón very well, the two horses Gerard had traveled abroad to buy, and that the differences in performance were notable. While one was among the best horses of the last ten years, Lebón, after his first three wins, had drastically lowered his performance due to a serious injury and respiratory issues that had turned him into a 'roarer' horse.

AP Photo

Horseracing journalist Julian Perez, of Uruguay, strokes the muzzle of the horse believed to be the stakes-winner Cinzano at Gambeling Farms, where it is staying. Kathy Morrison, farm manager, steadies the horse.

Uruguayan journalist Julián Pérez with Cinzano in the United States. Photo: AP, published on *Newsday* on September 14, 1978.

Dr. Manuel Gilman gave his statement on the same day, after some comings and goings with Bailey, since Bailey blamed his office for the whole problem with a not-so-subtle "you ruined everything". To this, Gilman gave him a serious look and responded "nothing was ruined here", without moving a muscle in his face. The doctor explained that when Lebón got to the track on the day of his debut, a NYRA official by the name Frederik Berlew had noticed that the import certificate described the mark on the head as a 'white star,' which did not match the white star with a stripe extending under the eyes of the horse he was examining. Berlew had passed the problem onto him, and he had gone to the Jockey Club to compare the photos taken of the supposed Lebón on the track with those in the Jockey Club's registration file. Since the track photos matched the ones on file, he decided that the description on the import certificate was incorrect, not knowing that Gerard had registered the horse with the Jockey Club and had also provided photos. He continued his account by recalling that in the past twenty years, they had stopped twenty-four attempts at swapping horses before the races, "Yes, yes, fine... but you missed this one," Bailey retorted.

The other interviewee of the day was the billionaire Joseph Taub. The owner of the Nets franchise confirmed that he had worked with Dr. Gerard on more than twenty thoroughbred racehorse acquisitions. Regarding the events, he acknowledged that the veterinarian had called him on June 13, 1977, to inform him of Cinzano's accident, and that he had subsequently instructed his employees to manage the horse's life insurance claim. The prosecutor tried to strike at his ego by asking if he knew he had paid $162,000 for a horse that had cost $81,000, but Bailey objected, mentioning taxes and the cost of transporting the animal, so Davenport reluctantly withdrew the question.

On September 14, Dr. Hemphill and trainer Joseph

McMahon took the stand. The latter testified that Gerard had hired him to train the horse that would eventually come to win in Saratoga. When signing the agreement, Gerard had told him that the horse was four years old but didn't reveal the name. The horse had arrived at the stud with a bridle marked 'Lake Delaware,' he referred to him as Denim, and after going every day in August to closely monitor the horse's progress, McMahon confirmed that his name was Lebón.

The veterinarian had a tougher time than the previous witness. For starters, he was in trouble for signing the death certificate, so he traded his testimony for immunity. As his presentation before the jury, he confessed to having certified Cinzano's death without ever having seen the horse, since the night of June 12, 1977, he had not gone over to Dr. Gerard's farm. He had even signed Cinzano's life insurance claim. "Gerard has everything, he doesn't need a scam," he thought. Besides, everyone knows the phrase that causes all trouble: "Sure, I'll do it. No one ever finds out." I have no proof, but I also have no doubt that Hemphill said this during the June 12 phone call. The only thing he saw, as did everyone else, was a picture of a broken leg, which, supposedly, belonged to Cinzano. From the moment the rumors started going around regarding an alleged horse trade performed by Gerard, Dr. Hemphill's lawyer suggested that he record all the conversations he had with his famous colleague and, if worse came to worse, tell the truth to all the investigators. This advice was followed religiously, and the jury had the opportunity to listen to Dr. Gerard urging him in two separate occasions, to remain true to the original story, to confirm to the authorities that he had gone to Muttontown on the night of June 12. He definitely set Mark up. "Hang in there, if you change your story, this will become a snowball that will drag us all into the horror," were, more or less verbatim, the words uttered. And I say more or less because nuance can be lost in translation, not because I am exaggerating or making things up.

Bailey was taken aback upon hearing those tapes and asked the judge to dismiss them, but he was unsuccessful. He then tried to go after Hemphill, accusing him of recording the conversations and coaxing Gerard into talking to save his own skin. However, the veterinarian stood his ground and weathered the storm.

On Friday, with the testimonies from the racetrack's cashiers, a week that had become highly favorable for the prosecution thanks to the recordings came to an end. The first to testify was Gerald Rosenwasser, who saw Gerard approach the betting windows on three separate occasions. Adding up all his trips, he had wagered a total of around $1,500 on Cinzano/Lebón/Denim. Next up was Philip Gianne, who stated that, after the race that Lebón had won, the man seated in front of him that day, wearing a brown jacket, had stood at his window and asked:

"— Do you already know what the payout's gonna be?

— No, but it's going to be crazy.

— Then have someone bring you more money."

After that phrase, Billy Anderson appeared on the scene—an ex-jockey who had known Gerard for twenty years and now worked as a cashier at Belmont Park—coincidentally at the window next to Philip Gianne's.

"—Hi, Mike, did you place some bets on this horse?

— No, I was just teasing your partner."

After his response, Gerard bolted faster than lightning to find another window where no one knew him. He chose Thomas DiBlasi's window, who recalled him placing $77,920 in a brown paper bag and handing it to the man. However, he hadn't gotten a good look at him because he was too focused on requesting more cash and validating the thirty-two $50 tickets Gerard had handed over (twenty-six for a win and six for a show). If any were fake or incorrect, DiBlasi would have had to cover the error out of his own salary. He mentioned that he had asked a Pinkerton guard to escort him to the exit, but the veterinarian had refused, a fact corroborated in court by the security guard: "He brushed me aside with his arm, tucked the bag under his arm, and left for his car in a hurry."

Vaya semanita (Translator's Note: *Vaya semanita* roughly translates as "What a week.") was the name of an excellent comedy show from the Basque Country, and it was likely also the phrase Bailey muttered as Friday came to a close. During the cashiers' testimonies, his only move was to crack a joke with Thomas DiBlasi about the tip the lucky bettor might have left him. His focus, however, was on the trial's final week and the testimony of Alice Gerard, who was expected to incriminate herself to save her husband's neck.

Let's take advantage of the fact that this account has brought us to the second weekend of the trial and take a judicial pause ourselves. Let's go back to Saturday, September 16, a day that marked a historic moment for American and global horse racing. On the dirt track of Belmont Park, the last two Triple Crown winners faced off: the colt Affirmed, champion of the current year, against Seattle Slew, the star of 1977. The 1,800 meters of the Marlboro Cup (Grade 1) bore witness to a unique, thrilling, and probably once-in-a-lifetime event (the closest comparison being Man O'War vs. Sir Barton in the early 20th century). The winner, leading from start to finish, was Seattle Slew, but his defeated rival left everything on the track, elevating the achievement even further. If you can, look up the race on YouTube and crank up your speakers—the roar of the crowd still gives you goosebumps.

The Monday following the aforementioned duel marked the start of the trial's final week, with all the pressure falling squarely on F. Lee Bailey, whose defense strategy had been shattered by the tapes and the testimonies of the racetrack cashiers. All signs pointed to the day's star witness being Alice Gerard, the veterinarian's wife, temporarily separated (according to the official version) and the scapegoat of the defense. Alice was a former teacher in her early thirties at the time, with nine years of marriage to Dr. Gerard and a decade of psychiatric treatment under her belt. After her preliminary statement before the grand jury in February, she had undergone two voluntary hospitalizations in New York and Connecticut, before relocating to California.

She got to the building, crossed herself, prayed on her knees on the steps, and entered the courtroom with her usual elegance. Her lawyer, Stephen Peskin, had managed to delay her appearance in court until Monday, September 18, but he needed one more day to continue studying the testimony Mrs. Gerard had given in February. He questioned the scope of the immunity agreement that Bailey had mentioned, as, in his view, his client could still be liable for criminal charges if she maintained her preliminary statement. At the same time, he took a jab at his colleague, saying that "Bailey's analysis of New York law leaves much to be desired." Prosecutor Davenport supported the defense attorney, saying that Alice Gerard would not be prosecuted for any crimes stated before the grand jury, but the judge granted Peskin's request, and the testimony was delayed for at least another twenty-four hours.

It seemed that Monday, without the defendant's wife on the stand, would be uneventful, but the prosecution presented Phillip Maxwell as a surprise witness. He was a racetrack employee working as a betting window runner, who had previously worked as an exercise rider many years ago. "I've been in the racing business since 1947, and I've known Dr. Gerard since around 1952, back when he was a young man trying to make a buck at the racetrack and its surroundings." On September 23, Maxwell was working as a messenger, just like any other day, when DiBlasi surprised him with a request: "Bring me $75,000." He went to the room where the money was stored, requested the sum, and returned to the window. According to him, he usually never paid attention to the bettors, but in this case, curiosity got the better of him, and he peeked to see who the lucky winner was. "I saw Dr. Gerard," he said.

"Is that person here in the courtroom?" the judge asked. Maxwell seized the opportunity to put on a little performance that had everyone in the room in giggles. First, he started scanning the jurors and shaking his head as if to say "no". Then he moved on to the reporters, repeating the gesture. He craned his neck to look at the audience, and at that point, Bailey, seeing there were no other options, stood up with a smile and raised his right hand. Next to him, Mark Gerard also stood up, smiling, and waved to the witness. Maxwell immediately responded, "Ohhh, Doc! It's you! Still the same!" Then, turning to the jury, he added, "He hasn't changed a bit, has he? Still looking good."

He closed his statement by recalling the conversation he had with Gerard while the latter was cashing in the tickets:

"—Why did you bet on this horse?

— I had a dream."

Tuesday was "D-day" for the defense. It was finally time for Alice Gerard's statement, and the fate of the most famous veterinarian in the world hanged on it. The defense's third and final witness entered the courtroom looking even more striking than the day before. A chorus of hushed voices and gazes from the crowd followed her as she made her way to the stand. Once the room fell silent, Alice took the oath and sat down to deliver the testimony that could save Mark Gerard from seven years in prison.

She began by saying what was expected—that she had harbored a long-standing animosity toward the Jockey Club and the NYRA for their insensitive treatment of horses: "I tried to show them that, just once in their lives, they could make a mistake and lose that callous and arrogant attitude." Based on that sentiment, she explained, she had planned the horse switch entirely on her own. The idea was hers, and she carried it out without ever telling her husband. She traveled to South America specifically to choose a horse that resembled Cinzano, switched the horses on June 11 when they arrived at Muttontown, and the next day, "there were a dozen cats chasing a rabbit. Lebón got scared, reared up, hit his head, and broke a leg in the fall," she said through genuine sobs. "With what I'm saying, I hope they'll stop blaming my husband. I only wanted to show them they could be wrong at least once," she added, with less sincerity than in her earlier statement. She concluded her testimony by admitting to the acts she allegedly carried out and accepting the consequences they might bring her (although, with immunity in place, it's easy to play the hero):

"I never told the authorities because I didn't know my husband would be accused of the crime," declared Alice Gerard, adding yet another layer of drama to her testimony. Then, as if she hadn't delayed her appearance at every opportunity since being asked to testify, she added with apparent conviction: "I was willing to testify with or without immunity. Guilt is a terrible burden to live with; it was driving me crazy."

After her testimony concluded, Bailey dismissed her without asking any questions, but then prosecutor Davenport stepped in, having sharpened his teeth as he listened. From the outset, he went straight for the jugular, accusing her of killing Lebón as part of the plan. "I'm a vegetarian; I don't eat meat. I would never be involved in the killing of a horse," Alice defended herself through sobs, unable to hold back her emotions whenever Lebón's death was mentioned.

Alice Gerard

Alice Gerard on the day of the preliminary hearing. Photo: *Daily News*

One of the most laughable moments of the cross-examination came when the prosecutor reminded her that, on the day of the horse's debut, she had bet $7,000 on it to win. "Were you really trying to get back at the NYRA and the Jockey Club, or did you do all this for money?" Mrs. Gerard, her voice initially steady but eventually breaking, responded that she had everything—"from a Jaguar to anything you could imagine; I had all the material things I wanted." Through tears, she offered the excuse of the decade: she had bet $7,000 because if she won, she was planning to "start a horse protection society for racehorses."

Towards the end of his cross-examination, Davenport, whose body language could not conceal his defeat, tried to make a last-ditch effort and asked Mrs. Gerard if she was also responsible for the other two alleged changes of thoroughbreds imported by her husband. This surprised everyone in the courtroom, even Bailey, who jumped to his feet objecting to the question. But the judge ignored him, and Harrington allowed Alice Gerard to consult with her attorney outside the courtroom on how to respond to this part of the questioning. Since the immunity only applied to the Cinzano-Lebón case and did not cover the other two horse switches (Enchumao-As de Pique and Chirico-Sundoro), Peskin advised his client to invoke the Fifth Amendment and refrain from answering anything that could harm her. The Fifth Amendment, among other things, states that no one shall be compelled to testify against themselves in a criminal case, so Mrs. Gerard found it quite convenient to avoid answering questions that would likely overturn the favorable outcome of her testimony up until that point.

For Bailey, the wife's testimony "was even better than expected." Mark, in the height of popularity, also gave interviews to reporters. Did he thank his wife for sacrificing herself? Not a chance, this was the '70s, and he only had praise for his lawyer: "Bailey gave a master class, today the trial took a favorable turn. I feel fantastic."

On September 20, F. Lee Bailey and Thomas P. Davenport presented their closing arguments for the defense and the prosecution, respectively. The courtroom was more crowded than usual, so the court officials had to bring in extra chairs. According to journalists, there were between one hundred and one hundred and eighty people waiting for the closing statements, which, by the way, were far from those of Perry Mason. Instead, they were a rather boring and, obviously, biased summary of the trial.

During the seventy-five minutes in which Lee Bailey addressed the jury, he emphasized two key points that they should keep in mind: Alice Gerard's confession, and the false testimony (in his view) of trainer Jack Morgan. "He was the only one who committed perjury in this courtroom," the lawyer said as he reminded the six men and six women of the jury that the prosecution had based its accusations on a witness who (according to him) had lied under oath. He also urged them to privately ask themselves if "the story of Mrs. Gerard could be true." If they believed that, they should look no further, because in that woman's "moderately unstable" sincere confession lay the salvation of his client.

The prosecutor was harsher than the day before with Alice

Gerard; he accused her of creating an atmosphere "similar to a circus" with her testimony and said:

> I didn't dare attack this poor woman. I think she is a pathetic person, but she is not credible. I think she is a sad person, but she is not credible. Her entire account is a work of fiction. It would insult your intelligence to ask that you believe her.

After these acrid words, Mrs. Gerard jumped from her seat, threw Davenport a fiery glance and stormed out of the room like a whirlwind.

He never stopped reminding the jury that the only person responsible for the fraud was Mark Gerard and that greed had been the motive. "You have the chance to deliver justice; if you allow yourselves to become the final victims of Dr. Gerard's trick, we will have lost something today." With that statement, the state's representative concluded his argument and handed the case over to the jury.

After the closing arguments, Alice Gerard approached her husband, and they were seen chatting amicably before heading off for dinner. They had been careful not to be seen together during the trial, but now that the jury was deliberating, they could return to normal.

THE VERDICT

What seemed like a quick decision turned out not to be, as the jury requested to review a couple of statements. The first was from one of the defense witnesses, trainer Howard Hessen, who had testified that he couldn't identify the deceased horse because it was covered in lime. Gerard insisted the horse was Cinzano.

That was two hours into the deliberation. After reviewing that statement, they requested to hear Gerard's testimony before the New York Racing and Wagering Board again, where he declared that he could easily identify the two horses involved. Those recordings lasted ninety minutes and were completed by eleven p.m., which prompted Judge Harrington to order that the twelve jurors spend the night in a hotel, completely isolated, to resume their task the following day. The twenty-five individuals still in the courtroom received the news with annoyance and left the premises with a mix of frustration and exhaustion.

On the morning of September 21, the jury reconvened, but they were far from reaching a verdict. They even requested another testimony to be reread; this time, it was that of James MacMahon, the trainer at the Saratoga Race Course. MacMahon had stated that Gerard had brought him a horse under the name Lake Delaware, which later became Denim, and that, finally, when he moved it to the stables at Belmont

Park, he had acknowledged its name was Lebón.

Above, the four people involved in the trial. Below, the jury en route to a hotel to spend the night before issuing the verdict. Facsimile: *Newsday*.

This witness was the prosecution's strongest, as he made it clear that Gerard did not want the true identity of the mysterious horse to be known. If he had been so certain it was Lebón, he wouldn't have gone to such lengths to create a spectacle around its identity. Searching the Equibase records, I found that no horse named Denim had been active in the United States, and the only one by the name Lake Delaware had ended its racing career in 1970. So, for once, it wasn't about changing identities but rather keeping the qualities of his thoroughbred under wraps. This jury request left the defense team visibly nervous, which was especially noticeable during the lunch break. They knew Mark Gerard's fate hinged on the persuasive power of the jurors who believed this witness versus those who believed Alice. There was no other possible outcome.

The clock marked 3:45 p.m. when the jury announced they had reached a verdict, and heartbeats were racing as in the final moments before the start of a race. The tension was palpable, the air so thick it could be cut with a knife, as the reading began:

> "—On the two charges of fraudulent practices in racing competitions, we find the defendant… guilty.
>
> On the charge of forging a commercial record, we find the defendant… not guilty.
>
> On the charge of forging an insurance claim, we find the defendant… not guilty.
>
> On the charge of horse theft to Mr. Joseph Taub, we find the defendant… not guilty.
>
> On the charge of theft to Lloyd's London insurance company, we find the defendant… not guilty."

The jury's decision took everyone by surprise; it was a 1.50 odds bet that Gerard would be convicted on all charges, and not even the most optimistic member of F. Lee Bailey's team had dreamed of this verdict. He was acquitted of all major charges and convicted on two minor ones, going from a probable sentence of nineteen years in prison to a maximum sentence of two years. The courtroom was buzzing, journalists scrambled to relay the news to headquarters and interview the key figures to get an exclusive. As Alice Gerard left the courtroom, her eyes filled with tears, she attempted to hug her husband, but she never made it as both were surrounded by reporters firing questions like machine guns.

"I don't think I saved my husband's reputation; I think I ruined his life," she replied when asked whether her testimony had saved the veterinarian's career. He couldn't hide his joy, wearing a grin from ear to ear, and it was no wonder; just moments before, there was a real possibility he would spend the next twenty years in prison, and he knew it better than anyone: "I thought it was going to be worse, that I was going to be the only victim in this case; my future was in the palm of their hands." He sent a brief message to the NYRA, assuring them they would have "a sense of satisfaction" from being convicted on two minor charges. "I would feel better if they hadn't convicted me of anything, but at least I'm not a horse thief. They used to hang them," he joked as he left.

His lawyer, F. Lee Bailey, was ecstatic as he stated:
"This was one of the strangest cases I've worked on. It's so

unbelievable, that a work of fiction with this plot would be turned down for being too far-fetched." He probably said that because it was still eighteen years before the O.J. Simpson case, and he didn't have a crystal ball. Bailey also mentioned that the jury's decision hinged on the moment when Gerard had learned about the switch, not whether he had orchestrated it; this showed that the jury had believed at least part of Alice Gerard's story. Despite the favorable outcome, the lawyer would go all in and appeal the conviction, as he didn't see the verdict as a total victory: "Because Dr. Gerard never admitted to racing the wrong horse," but he was nonetheless pleased that his client "didn't have to face twenty years in prison."

A source told us that a letter from Dr. Jorge Diehl from Argentina might have influenced the jury. In the letter, he supported the veterinarian, highlighting his professional qualities and personal charm. He expressed that, if it had been up to him, he would have continued negotiating with Dr. Gerard after the trial. We'll never know if that letter actually existed or if it's part of the many urban legends surrounding the case. I was surprised to hear that version after reading the note Dr. Diehl gave to the New York Times ten months before the verdict, but as Fox Mulder would say, "I want to believe."

Several members of the jury admitted that Mrs. Gerard's story was not entirely believable, but it had created reasonable doubt in their minds that perhaps she was the one responsible for the horse swap, and that was why they could not convict her husband. However, they had no doubt that Dr. Gerard knew the horse was Cinzano at the time he placed his bet on September 23.

The big loser of these sixteen days was prosecutor Thomas P. Davenport, who tried to explain to the press that the jury had accepted the idea that Gerard was involved in the horse swap, but for some reason, they were not convinced that he had also planned it. He claimed that the inconsistency in the verdict was due to the fact that there was no direct victim in this case. Come on, Thomas, admit it, you lost this one.

On the other hand, the president of the NYRA, James Heffernan, celebrated that the jury's position aligned with that of the organization by confirming that Gerard had knowingly raced the "wrong" horse. Although this alignment should have settled the matter, Heffernan, still holding a grudge against the veterinarian, declared that even if Mark Gerard were to receive a license to work from the New York State Racing and Wagering Board, the NYRA had the right to exclude him, as they were an independent body. They were even considering the decision to ban him from attending as a spectator at any of the three racetracks operated by the NYRA (Belmont Park, Saratoga, and Aqueduct).

The next day, at Belmont Park, the only topic discussed was Gerard's trial—the news of the moment. It was just one day away from the anniversary of Lebón's victory, and it coincided with the most bizarre event: Larry Adams, the jockey convicted as a sexual predator, had won a race in New York, his fourth that year. Everything came together so that everyone had their own theory about the case, and they were talking about it in the stands and in the locker rooms, between races. The jockeys generally agreed that Gerard had made the switch, since the defense had admitted it from the start. The trainers, who had worked most closely with the veterinarian, on the other hand, thought it was impossible that he was guilty, although the only argument they used was the trite "he's rich, he doesn't need a scam." They couldn't believe he would throw away his career and a $200,000-a-year income for a little extra money, even though the evidence was overwhelming. The NYRA was waiting for the first days of November, when Judge Harrington would issue the final sentence to revoke Gerard's veterinary license, as a criminal conviction was enough reason to revoke a professional's credentials, something they had hoped for ever since they had received the call from Uruguay nearly a year earlier.

Cinzano was actually yet another one to celebrate the end of the trial. On September 22, he was finally released after eleven months in hiding. His new/former owner, Jack Morgan, went to pick him up from the farm where the prosecution had kept him and took him to Meadow Hill Farm, where he would begin training for future competitions... Excuse me while I laugh, Jack, but I'm not really laughing at you, I'm laughing with you. It was pretty clear that, by regulation, they would never lift the suspension. Only Morgan and his lawyer believed there was a chance of reversing the decision made by the New York Racing and Wagering Board back in August. But hope springs eternal, and we'll support the old warhorse in his crusade, even though we have the benefit of hindsight. To be fair, the lawyer's argument wasn't bad, as it was based on the recently concluded trial, in which it was confirmed that the horse was indeed Cinzano. But he didn't count on the fact that this case had struck a nerve with the Jockey Club and the NYRA, injuring their pride and leaving them exposed. They wanted to erase any reminder of it from the face of the earth. In Cinzano's authorization, they had the regulation on their side, and no matter how confirmed his identity was, they only had to stick to the rules to achieve their goal.

On September 28, Morgan and his attorney appeared before Judge Burke to request an order forcing the New York racing authorities to allow Cinzano to race again. The judge denied the order, stating that it was still too early to make a decision and that they first needed to submit a formal request to the NYRA and the Racing and Wagering Board. The latter body had scheduled a hearing soon to address the case, according to its executive director, John Van Lindt, who, by the way, was covering himself by saying: "We need to determine if the identity of the horse is so unclear that the public won't know who they're betting on". Even though the District Attorney's Office and Mark Gerard himself agreed in the trial that the horse was indeed Cinzano, Van Lindt clarified, "This is not binding for our office." The die was cast, and all the key players, to varying degrees, knew it.

Things were fairly calm for over thirty days, until November 3, when Judge Harrington issued the sentence for Dr. Mark Gerard regarding the two lesser charges he had been found guilty of. There was some anticipation for the judge's decision, but it was nothing compared to the trial; the fact that twenty years in prison were no longer at stake removed the suspense, so when Harrington announced one year in prison and a $1000 fine, it didn't matter much to anyone outside of the interested parties. In his sentencing statement, he emphasized: "The message must be conveyed that individuals in his position who engage in this type of activity face substantial penalties so that they can consider the consequences of their actions; these penalties must deter them from such behavior."

Before the sentencing, prosecutor Davenport stated that there should be a prison sentence because "horse racing is an industry that provides entertainment to millions of people and generates significant income for the state; its integrity must be preserved." Fine speech, Mr. Prosecutor, but forty-five days earlier, you had everything in your favor to close the case and you let it slip away; the most dignified thing would have been to not say a word. Bailey defended his client and argued that a prison sentence would be excessive, "This is his first offense, he has heart problems, and he's already been punished for the entire year, as he was a respected veterinarian in the racing community, but that is long gone, his reputation is tarnished." As if we needed another sitcom moment in court, Judge Harrington had this conversation with Dr. Gerard:

"— Your last name is Geronimus?

— Yes, Your Honor.

— Geronimus, as in Louis Geronimus, the doctor who certified your heart problem in the parole report?

— Yes, he is my uncle."

Bail was set at $100,000 and would remain in place until November 9, the date when his appeal against the conviction would begin. For Mark Gerard, the conviction was a way to make an example out of him in front of the entire industry. According to him, a Sports Illustrated report that had been published that same week had a significant impact, as it discussed an ongoing investigation into a large number of jockeys accused of rigging races for substantial sums of money.

On November 13, the Jockey Club officially decided to suspend for life the other horses involved in the switches organized by Mark Gerard. Although the resolution included a confidentiality agreement with the owners of Chirico, Sundoro, and As de Pique, anonymous sources confirmed the matter to journalist Ed Comerford. The next day, Jack Morgan had a hearing in the Supreme Court, where he requested an order to force the NYRA to accept Cinzano at its racetracks, but... under the name of Lebón. After two months of saying that, according to the trial, everyone knew it was Cinzano and he went on to ask that it be called Lebón again; now I understand why the officials were completely ignoring him.

November 16 might have been Gerard's last victory of the year in court, as he succeeded in having the judge accept his request to delay the execution of his sentence and allow him to remain free until the resolution of the appeal in March 1979. That was also the last development in the case during a rather eventful year. For starters, it was claimed that the fire at the Hawthorne Park racetrack in Chicago in November had been set to erase evidence of other horse switches. The method of identifying thoroughbreds had been changed, and investigations into identity swaps of horses spanned six states. And finally, no one knew that Cinzano's fate was beginning to change, and that a new destination would bring him the glory he had once savored in Uruguay, a glory for which he was evidently destined.

LEGEND

The year 1979 started with good news for Cinzano since, thanks to tireless efforts, on Wednesday, January 17, the United States Supreme Court granted the appeal of the September 28, 1978 ruling, and forced the Jockey Club to immediately schedule a meeting with the aim of officially re-registering the horse and, in doing so, obtaining authorization for him to race again in U.S. racetracks.

This ruling gave hope to poor Morgan, who had acquired the Uruguayan star at that public auction after no one bid the $33,000 reserve price; a 'bargain' that wasn't, as he ended the year with debts exceeding $40,000 due to the upkeep of Cinzano and Blithe Reward, another horse he owned that had also been 'locked up' because it actually belonged to Mark Gerard.

After the initial, 1-month suspension in 1977, he was banned from entering his barn until well into the following year, something unheard of considering that his involvement in that instance was as a state witness.

A few days before the Supreme Court of Justice ruling, the caretaker gave an interview to the New York Daily News, in which he was still considering the possibility of a clearance:

> According to the Jockey Club, they are seriously considering Cinzano's return to racing, but they are asking me to castrate him. Why should I castrate him if the horse did nothing? Even the worst criminals aren't castrated. What did the horse do to deserve this? The situation has been stalled for some time now, and I don't have any more money to sustain this lawsuit. If it isn't resolved quickly, it could financially drain me.

The part about castration is somewhat colorful and shows a person who doesn't seem to have all their ducks in a row, but the reality is that Morgan was considering the possibility of selling him as a breeding stallion in Uruguay if he didn't get the clearance to compete in the U.S. Was this a real possibility or just a rumor? We'll never truly know because, a month after the article, the Jockey Club would definitively close the matter with a negative decision, and although Morgan would attempt a new appeal which was rejected on November 5, by the middle of that month, he would sell the horse to another optimist: David Denise. The price? $30,000—a solid deal.

I referred to David Denise as 'another optimist,' and the adjective suits him, as he paid three times more than what Morgan had 'paid' for a horse that couldn't run official flat races, but with the hope that the National Steeplechase and Hunt Association (NSHA) would not support the decision and would allow him to race officially in hurdle races.

I'll add a parenthesis to remind you that in this discipline, at the beginning of this century, the Uruguayan horse Inti (2005, Dubai Dust and Rigolina) stood out. He was exported to the United States after winning the 2007 Campeones Juveniles, fully taking advantage of the gold rush generated by Invasor's victories. His racetrack campaign didn't go well, as he ran seventeen times and couldn't win a single race. However, when he switched to hurdle races, he transformed, achieving three victories in sixteen appearances, including a Group 3 win in 2013 and a Group 3 placing in 2014.

Since mid-1979, Cinzano had been learning the craft of jumping at Randy Waterman's farm, a true star in the steeplechase and foxhunting scene in Virginia and Maryland. But before focusing on his new life as a jumper, let's review the year of the infamous Mark Gerard, who on June 11 received the news that the Brooklyn Court of Appeals had denied his request and upheld the September 21 ruling: one year in prison and a $1,000 fine. The veterinarian's ego needed absolution, and just a month after the ruling, he would file a new appeal against his conviction in the Albany courts (a sentence he was serving on bail thanks to a $100,000 bond). At the same time as the appeal, he requested a special permit from the Supreme Court to leave the country with the U.S. polo team, which was granted by the judge despite the prosecutor's objections, fearing a possible flight from the accused. The conditions of the permit were as follows: departure to Argentina on December 1, upon payment of $25,000, and return to the U.S. on December 10. The swindler, moving freely; the caretaker, counting lint in his pocket; and the horse, unable to race; it's not only in poor countries that we cut the chain at the weakest link.

As our main characters wandered among appeals, courtrooms and equine rehabilitation farms, alarms once again went off at the NYRA: a mare called Sandjoanbar, owned by Stanley Yagoda, was disqualified from a race on Saturday, July 21, at Belmont Park, because her physical characteristics did not match the description accompanying her registration. On Monday, July 23, they did a blood test to confirm that she was the daughter of Terra Firma, but the results yielded that this was not true either. The owner was furious: the five-year-old mare had run forty-six times and had passed through the hands of four owners, but only with him had they paid attention to those details. The thing, my dear Stan, is that the mare had never run in Belmont Park, and at that race track, since Lebón's victory, controls had become stricter than a new commissioner on the job. Experts did not blame the current owner but suspected that everything had started during the horse's first campaign, when its owner was David Harum (who, by this time, was serving a four-year prison sentence in New Jersey for fraud) and trained by William H. Rodgers, more famous for his sanctions than his victories. With them, the horse had won two of its three victories, and after leaving their hands, the campaign had plummeted to the cheapest claimings. What mare did Mr. Yagoda claim on May 7, 1979? We'll never know; or maybe we will, but the point is not to conduct that investigation, but simply show another example of a switch (as they called it in North America, referring to horse-switching) to contextualize the era and make it clear that the Lebón/Cinzano case was not an isolated event and that Mark Gerard was not the only one practicing these dishonest tactics.

By the year 1980, the horse had graduated to 'jumper' and the only thing left was for the NSHA to authorize its participation in races. However, since the decision was delayed, Denise entered him in amateur races at the Virginia Point-to-Point Circuit, which are held during the spring in the Northern Hemisphere. These races are cross-country events, featuring obstacles made from tree trunks, rocks, and small water puddles hidden behind the hurdles, along with steep ascents and descents. Cinzano made his debut on March 22 at the Piedmont meet, but his performance didn't meet expectations. He retired from the 2400-meter hurdle race, which was won by Royal Greed in a time of 4 minutes and 2 seconds. Like Cinzano, Royal Greed had raced at official tracks, but without much success—he only won once in his debut, which turned out to be his only victory throughout his campaign. Later, he would secure his one and only official win in steeplechase races. In the race program, Cinzano was listed as a six-year-old gelding, despite still being a 'sound' horse, with "NNP" next to his name. This acronym, often seen in race programs at smaller tracks, stands for "No Name Pedigree", a label that is unfair and likely unfamiliar to newer generations.

On April 5, Cinzano participated in the Old Dominion meet, listed for the sixth race over a 3200-meter course. This time, his performance was solid, as he finished second behind El Diento, who completed the distance in 3 minutes and 55 seconds. After two and a half years without competing, the uruguayan champion was getting into shape and a week later would confirm its status by obtaining its first victory at Oatlands over a distance of 2800 meters. In this race, Cinzano left his closest rivals far behind. His immediate competitors were Potter Street, a racehorse with a mediocre track record, and Blue Barbizon, a winner of fourteen races and nearly $100,000 in earnings, who had even competed in group-stakes events. Despite Blue Barbizon's impressive credentials, neither could keep up with Cinzano, who completed the 3200-meter race in 3 minutes, 13 seconds, and four-fifths, a full four seconds faster than the other race held over the same distance.

Although this triumph had no repercussion whatsoever (*The Baltimore Sun* listed the horse as 'Cinvano'), it was major for two reasons: it began a streak of twelve consecutive wins that kept him undefeated for three years, and was the final race under the ownership of David Denise.

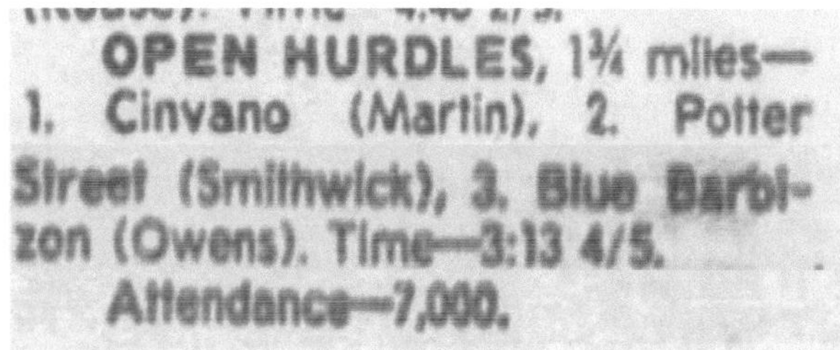
OPEN HURDLES, 1¾ miles—
1. Cinvano (Martin), 2. Potter Street (Smithwick), 3. Blue Barbizon (Owens). Time—3:13 4/5.
Attendance—7,000.

Just as Maradona was humorously dubbed "Caradona" in his early press mentions, here, Cinzano became Cinvano. Facsimile: *The Baltimore Sun*..

Ten days after his victory, the NSHA ruled negatively on the Cinzano case, with only two board members voting in favor of officially authorizing the horse, one of them being Randy Rouse. Visibly upset with the decision, Denise made the following statement to the New York Times:

> I bought the horse with the intention of racing him, perhaps naively. I have his Uruguayan papers, and no one in the world doubts that this is Cinzano—except for the Jockey Club and the NSHA. Dr. Manny Gilman (veterinarian examiner for the NYRA) traveled to Uruguay, compared the horse's official description with his own observations, spoke with the former owner, his Uruguayan trainer, and the jockeys who had ridden him, and testified under oath that the horse I have is the original Cinzano.

With regards to Rule 10.5, which establishes that a horse competing under a name other than the one registered should be disqualified, Denise states the following:

> My lawyer tells me it did not violate number 10.5. He was never registered in this country, therefore he did not have a name registered here. He did infringe number 10.6, which establishes that if a horse is involved in a scandal, the commissioners may suspend it. That indeed happened, he was suspended for two years.

Denise stated that he ran the horse in the point-to-point circuit for fun, as he had nothing else to do with him. "He's a good horse," he said, "and I'm sure the racing public would enjoy seeing him. But I'm not sure what to do in the future." The same article lists the reasons why the horse could not compete officially, according to the authorities:

- No animal named Cinzano had been registered in the Jockey Club because the only one with that name was listed as deceased.
- Although the Jockey Club believed that that horse was Cinzano, there was no way of confirming his pedigree.
- Rule 10.5 was very clear: any horse running under a different name would be disqualified for life.

With this scenario, the future Denise was referring to needed to arrive as soon as possible. The point-to-point season was coming to an end, leaving no opportunities for the horse to race, even for fun, until the following year. As a result, Denise put the horse up for auction with a starting price of $15,000, but the attempt was unsuccessful. When the auctioneer dropped the price to $10,000, a buyer stepped forward: Randy Rouse. Yes, the very same person who had voted to approve the horse's eligibility in the NSHA and was already familiar with it from Randy Waterman's farm. He would personally take on the task of giving the horse the opportunity that the authorities had denied it. This horse was destined to become a legend, and three years after its fall from grace, it found refuge with another legend.

Randolph Dashiell Rouse was a veritable personality in the state of Virginia, not only as a foxhunter and amateur rider, but also as a distinguished member of high society. He was born on December 30, 1916, into a family connected to agriculture. He learned to ride in the company of his grandfather, and he quickly fell in love with horses. After graduating from Lee University, he began working in construction until the arrival of WWII. During the conflict, he served in the Navy offices in Washington, D.C., and, at the end of the war, he saw the business opportunity better than anyone else: he bought very cheap land and started building houses for soldiers returning as heroes from the battlefield. Evidently, he made quite some money, and continued to expand his business model throughout the region, as he returned to his old passion: horses.

He started at the Fairfax Hunt Club, where, in addition to

practicing fox hunting, he participated in hurdle races, initially with little success due to his lack of experience. However, he quickly adapted to the level required by the competitions. While making a name for himself as a rider, he married actress Audrey Meadows, star of the 1950s series The Honeymooners. But in 1958, two years after the wedding, they divorced. After this failed commitment, Rouse fully focused on his business and horses, to the point that he spent nearly twenty-five years without a partner. He himself referred to this period, admitting that he had to make a change in his life because he had become a "peculiar and undesirable" man. This change led him to meet Michele O'Brien, his second and final wife, who was with him from 1983 until the day he died. Michele shared his passion for horses and even enjoyed the thrill of winning some races, riding Cinzano in the mid-1980s (we'll get to that, don't worry.)

During the twenty-five years that Randy Rouse competed in the Virginia Point-to-Point Circuit, he won the Seven Corners Championship eleven times and the Casanova Cup thirteen times, in addition to experiencing a few falls and several fractures. He retired 1983, riding Cinzano, but continued as an owner and caretaker for another thirty-three years. His last official victory came with the horse Hishi Soar in an allowance optional claiming race held at Foxfield on April 30, 2016, at ninety-nine years old. As if that weren't enough, after turning one hundred, he delighted in achieving a win in the Virginia Circuit, again as owner and caretaker. That would be his final victory, as on April 7, 2017, three months after his birthday, he passed away at the Virginia Hospital Center.

According to Equibase, as an owner, he officially participated in 986 races, with 169 wins, 148 second-place finishes, and 135 third-place finishes. As a trainer, his record stands at 71 wins, 67 second-place finishes, and 84 thirds in 768 appearances.

After introducing its last owner, we go back to 1980, with the horse now at Rouse's estate. There, in addition to racing during Virginia's spring meetings, he lived the life of any other country horse: one day herding 150 cows, the next, winning by 25 lengths in Casanova. When he returned to the ranch, he would join Randy and his friends on hunting trips or be showcased at a dinner with politicians and diplomats. A true dandy.

Things weren't going so well for Mark Gerard, as on Friday, June 6 of that same year, the Albany Court of Appeals rejected his appeal and confirmed that there was enough evidence to uphold the conviction. The guy was determined not to go to jail, so a week later, his lawyers submitted a medical report claiming that prison was not a suitable place for his heart problems.

On Tuesday, June 17, Judge Raymond Harrington denied the request, but the parties involved appealed the decision before Friday, June 20 (the date set for his incarceration). The argument from his lawyer, Neil Shayne, about the veterinarian's health issues convinced Judge Frank Gulotta of the Nassau Appeals Division, who signed off on allowing the sentence to be served under house arrest. According to his lawyer, Mark Gerard had a progressive heart condition, and going to jail could result in his death in the near future. That "progressive condition" allowed the swindler to live just thirty-six more years. His lawyer? Nothing short of a genius.

The year 1981 was the year of the first season of the Rouse-Cinzano partnership. Registered under the owner-rider category, they had their debut in the Casanova Cup on February 28 and, being Randy a higher profile character than David Denise, the press was there in the racecourse this time around. And there was also a large crowd that had come solely to see Cinzano. The race was contested over 4,000 meters with wooden hurdles, stone walls, and water jumps. It featured six participants but only one star: Cinzano. From the start, he set the pace; three fences before the finish, he accelerated at his rider's request and left Chadds Ford (a winner of two races at racetracks with stakes placings) twenty lengths behind. He completed the distance in 5 minutes, 36.4 seconds.

Cinzano and Randy Rouse, 1981. Photo: Douglas Lee.

After the race, his owner declared that earlier that same Saturday morning, he had ridden the horse for five hours on a hunt and that the only preparation for the race had been a light workout over a mile in 1 minute, 58 seconds. With such a display, it was hard to imagine the duo facing any setbacks that year, and their rivals felt the same. A week later, only three dared to challenge them at the Rappahannock meet. There, Cinzano crushed his competition over 4,000 meters in the Ben Venue Cup, clearing all fourteen fences in 4 minutes, 52 seconds, finishing twenty lengths ahead of Boca Bird (Virginia Steeplechase hall of famer since 2011).

A week later, they repeated their success at the Blue Ridge meet by claiming the George P. Greenhalgh Memorial over 4,800 meters against a field of five competitors. On March 22, the pair triumphed again in the Potomac Cup, also over 4,800 meters, finishing in 5 minutes, 1.2 seconds—a time that allowed them to clearly outpace Gentleman Pro, Saint Denis, and two other rivals. With this victory, they secured the 1981 owner-rider category title. This win inspired a lengthy feature by journalist Vicky Moon for The Washington Post:

> Randy Rouse paced back and forth atop a hill at Woodley Farm, the 40-mph winds whipping through a thin layer of his red, white and blue racing silks.
>
> The start of the race had been delayed to allow an ambulance crew to remove a rider injured in a fall during the previous race. "This is ridiculous," said Rouse, 64, slapping a riding whip against his boots. "This is the only time I get nervous."
>
> His horse was being walked around the paddock. The big bay gelding was not as nervous as his rider. At age 7 he has seen it all. And more. Several hundred spectators, who braved near-freezing weather, leaned over a snow fence to get a close look at the horse. An oddsmaker, carrying a portable blackboard, barked, "Make

your bets here on the famous Cinzano."

The odds for the George Greenhalgh Memorial, a three-mile race over timber, were 1 to 8. They contrasted markedly to that September day in 1977 at Belmont Park, when Dr. Mark Gerard, a New York veterinarian who owned Cinzano, entered the horse under the name of Lebon. The $2 bettors collected $116 on the 57-to-1 shot.

[…]

Cinzano, a stakes winner in Uruguay, also is running free, making the rounds on the Seven Corners point-to-point circuit. And making them very quickly.

Rouse and Cinzano have won the season's first four races, at Casanova, Rappahannock, Berryville and Ptoomac last Sunday. There are 10 races for "gentlemen members of an organized hunt" in the Seven Corners Championship and Rouse has been master of the Fairfax Hunt since 1961. The winners each week are awarded points toward an end-of-season championship and the season. The champion buys dinner for the other members.

In the 20 years of the Seven Corners series, Rouse has picked up nine dinner checks. He heads the list in number of career wins with 52. He holds the top three positions in the leading horse standings over the years with three different horses. On Sunday, Cinzano will race for the last time this season at the Fairfax point-to-point, and a victory would clinch the Seven Corners for Rouse once again.

Cinzano is able to run at the point-to-point races (where a silver plate is awarded instead of money) even though he has no papers from The Jockey Club. At steeplechase races sanctioned by the National Steeplechase and Hunt, he needs to have the papers. The Jockey Club so far has declined to provide those papers for the horse's previous owner, David Denise of New Jersey.

"I don't understand if the trial proved that the horse was Cinzano, why nobody has been able to get the papers," Rouse said. But I bought the horse to hunt and ride point-to-point so I knew what I was getting. They started out asking $15,000 for him but I waited until they came way down. I haven't applied for the papers yet. I figured it wasn't appropriate. Why penalize the horse?"

[…]

Papers or no papers, it doesn't matter to Rouse, an Arlington real estate developer. He is out to have a good time -- and to win. He is concerned about the competition this day. There are two other horses entered who could set a quick pace. Too quick. Rouse doesn't want that. But they don't know it. So the riders play cat and mouse, checking the board to see if the other will perhaps scratch. There is always a chance of

> falling off. One false move or incorrect judgment while racing toward an unyielding four-foot timber fence at 30 mph results in horse and rider flipping over. In the 50-plus years Rouse has been riding, he remembers being knocked unconscious four times. Two years ago, he broke both ankles, when his mount stumbled over on top of him in heavy going. He rode again and won in seven months. Rouse fox hunts every chance he gets and jogs 30 minutes every day. Sometimes his friend and internist, Dr. Charles Waters Thompson, accompanies him to the races, just in case of another accident. "I'll probably retire next year", Rouse said. "But be sure to say probably".

With the Seven Corners Trophy in his pocket, the horse only needed to prove that he was on par with the best in the circuit. When the Fairfax meet in Leesburg arrived, Rouse decided to enter Cinzano in the unrestricted Open category and entrusted the ride to Donald Yovanovich. The result was the same as it had been all year: an easy victory over the fine Irish horse Red Invader (a winner of fourteen races at racetracks with some stakes shows) and Counterspy, with a time of 4 minutes, 9 seconds—the best of the afternoon.

By the end of the Virginia Circuit season, the horse had received three distinctions: Owner-rider Timber Champion, Leading Timber Horse, and Leading Horse over Fences. Meanwhile, his winning streak had reached six, and he marked a full year undefeated.

With all these accolades, in the fall of 1981, Randy Rouse decided that the audience deserved to see Cinzano once more before the '82 season. He entered him in a flat race over 2,400 meters on the turf at Fairfax, scheduled for September 26.

With Rouse himself in the irons, Cinzano stopped the clock at 2 minutes, 27 seconds, easily defeating the modest Salty Affair and Barbadou, to the ovation of the crowd. For a point of reference and to gauge the level at which he was competing, a 2,200-meter race was held the same day, won by Final Spring, a claiming horse, in 2 minutes, 15.4 seconds. The key difference? Final Spring was ridden by a professional female jockey, while our protagonist had an amateur jockey aboard, far from the usual weight of a professional rider.

The second chance life was giving Cinzano contrasted with the news about Mark Gerard that came out that same year. Two sides of the same coin—the facts only served to confirm how unjust the sanction had been. "Ball don't lie," as Rasheed Wallace would say. A month after the horse's last victory at Fairfax, Meadowlands Racetrack made headlines by revoking the racing registration of the Uruguayan horse As de Pique II. It turned out the horse was actually the Argentine Enchumao, both imported to the United States by Mark Gerard, as mentioned in the previous chapter. This sanction from the New Jersey racetrack was added to the one the horse already had in New York, which is why it had been out of competition since 1977.

As de Pique II, previously discussed in earlier pages, had been purchased by Joe Weiser in May 1981. He personally set to work preparing the horse to race that October. After a four-year absence from the track, the task was more than challenging, but we horse racing enthusiasts cling to any glimmer of hope, no matter how small. This hope was dashed before the start: the stewards requested that the horse be withdrawn, as their investigation had revealed that it was not the Uruguayan As de Pique II, but rather Enchumao.

The 1982 season was a carbon copy of the previous; the only notorious difference was the absence of press coverage. The horse had stopped being a novelty for those not acquainted with the sport, but he continued to be the star of the state of Virginia. According to Randy Rouse himself, Cinzano's presence doubled attendance at the point-to-point races, and it was very common to hear admiring shouts like, "We love you, Cinzano," as the dark bay raced across the tracks.

The campaign began with a decisive victory in the Casanova Cup, where Cinzano achieved the double event. That afternoon, a local TV channel filmed the event with plans to create a documentary about point-to-point racing. One of the cameramen asked who he should bet on, and a good Samaritan told him, "On Cinzano." The young man looked for the horse he was supposed to put his money on and felt disheartened when he saw the jockey: "I'm supposed to bet on that old guy?" Despite his prejudice, he followed the tip and placed his wager. When he saw the running machine that Cinzano was and how perfectly he and his jockey worked together, he couldn't believe it. After crossing the finish line, the cameraman went to share the story with Rouse, and the veteran couldn't help but laugh along with him.

Cinzano and Randy Rouse, 1982. Photo: Douglas Lee.

The following week, Cinzano also won his second Ben Venue at Rappahannock, but this time only by ten lengths, against the daring Worthy of Love, who managed to take the lead after the third hurdle (the race consisted of fourteen obstacles). However, once Rouse urged Cinzano to run, it was game over: he caught up with him, passed him, allowed him to regain hope, and then, after the final jump, comfortably pulled away again. The duo completed the two and a half miles in five minutes and five seconds.

Randy decided not to race at Blue Ridge and took a week off to aim for another double. This time, he achieved it with ease at the Potomac Cup on March 21. Just like the previous year, he wanted to test Cinzano against the best in the circuit, so he entered him in the Open Timber category without restrictions and entrusted his ride to William McCormick, a jockey and veterinarian by profession. The result? You won't believe it: another victory. He closed the championship with a win at the Oatlands meet, once again in the owner-jockey category, and secured the Seven Corners Trophy once more.

To celebrate the victory, two weeks later, Randy was at the door of a foxhunters' event. Politicians and diplomats were welcoming the guests; among them, as seen in the Washington Dossier, was Michele O'Brien, who would become Randy Rouse's wife. "I love it when a plan comes together," would say Hannibal Smith while chewing on a cigar.

A FOXY EVENING

Tally-ho was the byword as members and friends of the Fairfax Hunt gathered at the OAS Building for the annual Hunt Ball, benefiting the Pan American Development Foundation. Guests were greeted by (above) Huntsman Ian Milne, mounted on Cinzano, the outstanding point-to-point racer owned by Fairfax Hunt Master of Foxhounds Randy Rouse. Adding to the hunting atmosphere was

Despite the biting cold, Michele O'Brien, Va. Sen. Harry F. Byrd and Mass. Rep. Margaret Heckler cuddle in the antique carriage driven by Gail Conley and displayed outside the OAS Building at the Fairfax Hunt Ball.

Cinzano welcoming guests at the door and Michele O'Brien arriving to the party on a carriage. Facsimile: *Washington Dossier.*

I haven't forgotten about the awards collected in 1982, here they are: Timber Horse of the Year, Owner-Rider Timber Champion, Leading Timber Horse and overall Leading Timber Horse; the latter distinction included horses that could participate in official races. To close the calendar year, there was another victory at The Belmont meeting on September 25 at the Fairfax track, once again over 2400 meters, and once again with Randy Rouse in the saddle.

The year 1983 was a year of limited activity for two reasons. The first was at the request of the Virginia Point-to-Point Circuit organization. After winning the Casanova Cup for the third consecutive spring in a dominant fashion (once again leading from start to finish, taking 6 minutes and 05 seconds to cover the 17 obstacles of the 4000-meter course—his closest competitor arrived 32 seconds later), they asked Rouse not to enter him anymore in the owner-jockey category, which led Randy to confirm his retirement as a jockey with a personal record of 126 races, 56 wins, 25 places, and 12 shows. Together with Cinzano, they raced 12 times (9 with obstacles and 3 on flat ground) and won all 12—the perfect centaur.

The second reason was a chronic injury to a knee, which partly caused the first defeat in three years, also the first since Cinzano had come into Rouse's hands. The rider on that unfortunate afternoon in the 5200 meters of the Middleburg Bowl was William McCormick, who couldn't repeat the victory from the previous year. The winner was Chatex, a chestnut who had won four official races out of thirteen participations, and was ridden by Simon Shaw. The meeting also featured the Chilean horses Eden and Superior; the former finished as the runner-up to Tingles Image in a race reserved for losers, while his compatriot suffered an injury that prevented him from completing the Louis Leith Cup.

In 1984, the challenge was to recover from the last defeat and find his place in a new category—or rather two: lady jockeys and foxhunters. As expected, his debut took place on February 25 at the Casanova meet, but this time the chosen race was the Melrose Castle, a Lady Timber category event for female jockeys, spanning 4,000 meters. The uncertainty about how he would adapt to new hands lasted less than six minutes, as Toinette Jackson guided him to an effortless victory in 5 minutes and 48 seconds. Splashy Lea, ridden by Patti Cassel, came in second.

Cinzano and Rouse in action in the Casanova Cup of 1983. Photo: *Virginia Sportsman*.

Three weeks later, on March 17, he appeared at Warrenton to face the largest field of his career, with eleven rivals lining up against him in the three-mile Spring Road, another race reserved for lady jockeys. The rider changed, but the result did not, as Hilary Thompson followed in her predecessor's footsteps and won the race convincingly. Splashy Lea, once again ridden by Patti Cassel, finished second, and Handy Mill, a solid allowances horse from the 1970s, came in third.

Randy Rouse had reclaimed the champion, and to confirm the rising anticipation, he entered him in the Rokeby Bowl, the most prestigious race on the circuit. He once again entrusted the ride to William McCormick, who was eager for redemption, as he was the only jockey who had lost a race riding Cinzano since the horse joined Rouse's team. The veterinarian had sixteen years of experience as an amateur jockey, so that loss the previous year didn't weigh on him at all. Thanks to the internet, in 2013, I was able to get in touch with Dr. McCormick, who kindly sent me an email recounting his memories of the race:

> The Race:
>
> The race was the Rokeby Bowl. The silver bowl with many hallmarks was to be presented by sponsor Mr. Paul Mellon MFH (Master of Foxhounds), the owner of Rokeby Farm in Upperville Virginia, the center of foxhunting in Northern Virginia. Mr. Mellon was also a most prominent breeder of Thoroughbred race horses, including the winners of both the Kentucky Derby

(Sea Hero) and the Epsom Derby (Mill Reef); to this day Mr. Mellon is the only breeder to have accomplished this feat.

The winner of the Rokeby Bowl is usually the high point winner of the Virginia spring point to point circuit. Point to points are jumping races run over flagged courses at a distance of three to four miles over hunting countrys. The obstacles encountered would be those that one would expect to negotiate whilst out following hounds chasing a fox.

The Horse:

Cinzano, the object of this account, had endured a most circuitous route to become the favorite in the 1984 Rokeby Bowl. After his disbarment by the NYRA (New York Racing Association), Cinzano was acquired by Virginia horseman and successful amateur steeplechase rider, Mr. Randy Waterman, MFH. It was Mr. Waterman's intent to compete in sanctioned NSHA (National Steeplechase and Hunt) races. Unfortunately the most lucrative NSHA races were run at the summer meets sanctioned by the NYRA. The New York association understandably could not abide by this apparent attempt to evade its authority. There was little negotiation by the NSHA concerning the possibility of Cinzano, the ringer, competing in New York. Consequently, Mr. Waterman sold Cinzano to fellow Master of Foxhounds, Mr. Randolph Rouse.

The next three years Cinzano learned the skills of a field hunter, albeit a field master's horse. In the hierarchical structure of foxhunting, the field master's horse always leads the field of other participating riders and horses. Cinzano learned to relax in a field of horses, to negotiate all manner of ditches, streams, ground logs in the woods, stone walls, and board fences, i.e. essentially any obstacles that his rider wanted to jump. A point to point horse must learn to jump safely especially when tired. The master's horse must acquire the presence of mind to not run off, kick hounds or other horses.

The Rider:

In 1984, I had been riding in spring point to point races for the previous sixteen years. I had learned to ride at speed galloping racehorses for among others, Jonathan Sheppard, Tommy Field, Mrs. Sydney Watters, not to mention my father, James P. McCormick. My father had trained racehorses professionally since the collapse of the foxhunter market in the mid 1950's. Personally I regretted our move to flat racing, but I realized there was an opportunity to learn the skills of flat racing.

I had begun riding point to point races in the late 1960's whilst at college at the University of Virginia and subsequently as veterinary student at the University of Pennsylvania. Prior to 1983 I had ridden in four Rokeby Bowls, winning two and beaten a head in a third and one unplaced. I had met Randy Rouse during this time. When he needed an amateur rider for the 1984 Rokeby Bowl, I was available and more than willing to ride. In the previous year I had ridden Cinzano in The Middleburg Bowl, but the race had scratched down to two horses and was not much of a contest. Cinzano had never been beaten in owner rider races where the weight carried was higher than the Rokeby Bowl.

The Course:

The course was run over "fair hunting" country, meaning up and down hills over existing fence lines. The shape of the course was roughly an elongated dumbbell requiring right and left turns and passing the finish line three times. Cattle had grazed the course, but no farming had occurred for many years. The Wednesday before the race, three inches of snow had blanketed the course. As the snow slowly melted we were assured of having a soft course, as was the usual condition of spring point to points. Cinzano had good size feet, which would impart an advantage over smaller footed horses, especially in the deeper parts of the course.

The 3 1/2 mile course consisted of seven board or rail fences, 10 stone walls, an open ditch, two 90° turns both left and right, and a long 1/8th mile gallop downhill to a straight up and down 3 foot nine inch vertical stone wall. One would expect to run in less than 7:00 minutes i.e. a two minute lick. The course favored turning ability, tactical speed, clever as well as powerful jumping, and horses that preferred soft ground, and who were able to gallop up and down hills without losing stride rhythm.

The Race:

That day we had a glorious blue sky, and the temperature was about 55° F. The course was forgivingly soft after the snow on Wednesday. There was a full field of horses, one of which, Constantine, was a future near winner of the Virginia Gold Cup. Cinzano's former owner, Mr. Randy Waterman always a keen competitor, was riding Constantine. Cinzano looked like a champion in the paddock, while being walked by his groom Golden Thornton. The horse never turned a hair.

The race strategy was to take an early lead, let the horse settle in his stride, get a good unimpeded look at every fence, take advantage of sharp turns while in front, and be in position to sprint after the last stone wall (2nd to last fence about a ¼ mile from the finish).

When Cinzano had run at Middleburg the previous year, he had "lugged in" a bit at the end of the race. Also when he had won the "ringer race" in New York his jockey, Pete Anderson, remarked that Cinzano had lugged in. My guess is that Cinzano's left front fetlock had accumulated some damage over time. However, on the soft footing of the Rokeby Bowl, Cinzano travelled straight and true. He followed the plan to perfection. Not an inch of ground was lost on those 3 1/2 miles. We controlled the pace and led by five over the second to last. Mr. Waterman's Constantine was second in contention, but Cinzano sprinted to an easy ten length victory at the wire. It looked and felt very easy, but the planets have to be aligned for a perfect trip.

Conclusion:

It is hard to keep a good horse down. Cinzano won because he was a natural athlete with a big engine, and because he was properly and patiently prepared. A steeplechaser in essence is a speed horse that you can rate. With those qualities one must have jumping ability and athleticism. Cinzano could wrap around a tight turn like a hoop around a barrel. He jumped with great power and had the ability to leave out one or even two strides before a fence. Really he did not require much active riding just guidance, balance, and quiet hands.

My final thoughts were that Cinzano was the finest point to point horse that I had ever ridden. At the end of that year I would give up riding races after 16 years. I was 37 years old with a veterinary practice to attend to. Ultimately I knew that I would not likely ever have another such magical ride. Cinzano's and my best racing days came at the end of our careers. Tsun Tsu would say "the object of the struggle is victory not persistence."

Nothing more can be added after this beautiful memory

shared by Dr. McCormick, who, twenty days after the Rokeby Bowl, rode him again at Strawberry Hill when, seven years after the Belmont Park fraud, the horse returned to participate in an official event. On that April 14, several official races were held, but the one that drew the most attention from the press was the unofficial race, run over 4,400 meters with a prize of just $1,000. The day before the race, *Newsday* journalist Ed Comerford published an article titled "Cinzano Can't Run From Past Evil," which begins as follows:

> He is, in the testimony of everybody who has ever handled him, a lovable horse, combining an ideal temperament with an abundance of talent.
>
> He was, many years ago in a distant country, an idolized champion. But through no fault of his own he became an outcast, a pariah.
>
> His name is Cinzano. Saturday, in Richmond, VA, the dark-brown 11 years old gelding will appear at a sanctioned race meeting for the first time in seven years. But he not permitted to run in any of the big races at Strawberry Hill Hunts; just the opening race, purse $ 1,000 three miles over post-and-rail-fences.

In the article, we are introduced to a new villain named Bill Gallo. This figure, who at the time served as secretary of the NSHA, dismissively claimed that the horse would only be competing in that unofficial race and that, even if he won, the association would disregard it. However, as both the journalist and Randy Rouse rightly pointed out, no one was going to ignore him. With thirteen wins in his last fourteen races, he had already become a legend in the state of Virginia. "He doubles the crowd every time he runs. Everybody loves him, and they keep asking why he can't run in the big races," Rouse expressed, and mentioned that in some cases, the NSHA had lifted that suspension on horses "I rationalized that, since we permitted horses whose thoroughbred breeding could not be proved to compete in certain sanctioned hunts meeting races over timber, we could do the same for Cinzano." Gallo, a stickler for the rules, answered: "The rule is very clear. He's barred for life. Yes, we do allow that under extraordinary circumstances, maybe one or two cases a year, but never in cases like this, where the rule is clear and final."

With no way to measure himself against all the horses in the discipline, the question lingered: was Cinzano on par with the great official champions or not? Comerford asked Rouse about this, and he had no doubts on the matter:

> [He] is a lovely horse, just wonderful. And very smart. He understands fox-hunting is not competitive, so he relaxes; ladies have ride him. But when he knows it's a race, he take the bit and goes. I've had a lot of good horses, but Cinzano is in a class by himself. I don't think anybody could beat him. He's unreal.

But Bill Gallo did harbor doubts (and what wouldn't I give to tell him a few things face to face). For him, he would never become a contender for champion: "I've seen him jump, he's got the ability and he's very competitive, a tough *hombre*. But a championship contender, no." Yes, Bill, rest assured that we are going to believe in a sad bureaucrat such as yourself, than a guy who participated in almost a thousand races and cared for horses for over fifty years.

Excuse my anger, it won't happen again. To nobody's surprise, that day's victory went to Cinzano, and in the next day's edition of *Newsday*, the news was published with a title that settled the discussion: "Cinzano wins," ignoring the rest of the meet organized by the NSHA. Reality is the only truth, my dear Bill.

Seven days after this race, the horse wrapped up the season in Middleburg, finishing a distant fourth in a race about which we have little additional information. This lack of details was almost a constant throughout Cinzano's campaign in Virginia: if the horse won, the result would always appear in some newspaper, but on the rare occasions he was defeated, no one seemed interested in reporting it, as if the entire community refused to bring their hero down to a more earthly level. For them, Cinzano was unbeatable on and off the track, period.

In an article written by his sister, Parke, for the *Daily*

Press a month after that race, Randy himself stated that it was the best horse he had ever cared for in his entire life:

"The faster others go, the more he wants to go. And he goes at his own lick - he won't go slower. I wish he wouldn't go so fast. I'd like to be able to take him up to his fences a little more slowly, so we'd be less likely to fall, but he grabs the bit and there's no stopping him".

Cinzano and Rouse. Photo: *Daily Press* facsimile, June 3, 1984.

Unlike the period without distinctions in 1983, in 1984 he swept all the awards in the Virginia Point-to-Point Circuit. In the American amateur category, he was named Leading

Horse over Fences and Leading Timber Horse. In the unified category, encompassing both official and unofficial Virginia's races, he was also chosen as Leading Horse over Fences and Leading Timber Horse.

In 1985, he only ran one race: the three-mile Clark Courier Cup at the Blue Ridge meet, reserved exclusively for female jockeys. As expected, he claimed victory, this time under the guidance of Patti Cassel, who had trailed him twice the previous year. His time of 6 minutes and 21 seconds was remarkable compared to others recorded at that distance on the same day: 22 seconds faster than the novice category, 43 seconds faster than the owner-rider category, and 34 seconds faster than the open category. After the eight-length victory over Handy Hill, the jockey told *The Baltimore Sun*: "This horse is incredibly powerful; I was basically just a passenger the entire race." The newspaper's special correspondent noted that it was the fastest and most fiercely contested race of all those run over timber that day. Following this display, the organization once again requested Rouse not to enter him for the rest of the season, a request the owner graciously agreed to, prioritizing the sport's interests over his own.

Do you know who we haven't talked about for some time? Yes, Mark Gerard—the veterinarian who had been working with Miami-based polo teams, occasionally asking Rouse about Cinzano's knot—was back in the news. Was it for something good, like in his glory days? Of course not. It was due to suspicions that an Argentine mare named Computadora, racing at the California tracks, might belong to him. Since he was on bad terms with the NYRA, and by extension with West Coast authorities, he wouldn't be granted an owner's license. Additionally, as no veterinarian could officially be listed as a trainer under the rules, it was suspected he had resorted to the old trick of using figureheads. The listed owner was a New York lawyer named Mark Faden, who vehemently denied any connection to Gerard: "It's defamatory to suggest that Mark Gerard has anything to do with this mare. She is mine and mine alone." The suspicion arose because the mare's previous owner and trainer was a Florida woman named Ramona Smith, who (it was said) had a friendship with Gerard. In the East, the mare had raced three allowances, finishing second once. After those three races, she was sold to Faden for $70,000 through an intermediary. Her move to the West didn't suit her; in three races, she managed to beat only two rivals. This abrupt drop in performance raised alarms among the authorities, who immediately suspected some scheme involving the veterinarian. The case was closed without charges, and the mare reappeared the following year at Bay Meadows, a lower-tier track compared to California's main circuits. She ended her racing career that same year, adding two wins at Golden Gate to her record.

In 1986, the racetrack witnessed the first encounter

between Cinzano and Michele O'Brien Rouse, the wife of the legendary horseman. Although she had spent the entire year sharing hunts and rides with the horse, it wasn't until March 15, at the Warrenton meet, that she made her official debut with him. Specifically, it was during the Springs Roads Warrenton Hunt Cup, a race reserved for female jockeys, where our hero led the field from start to finish. He clocked 7 minutes and 3 seconds for the three miles, the best time of the day. The result of this race brought about the now-familiar request to Randy Rouse: "Please, don't bring him back." As Rouse himself admitted, whenever competitors learned that Cinzano was entered in a race, they would withdraw their horses. In the end, the only one negatively impacted was the sport itself. We'll uncover, in Michele's own words, what it was like to ride Cinzano at the peak of his career:

> You couldn't hold Cinzano in a race. Don't even try. He was so cool he'd walk around in the paddock beforehand as though he were asleep. Saunter down to the post on a loose rein. But oh wow, when the starter dropped the flag he was off like a shot. A front-runner wire to wire. Effortless, easy, cool. I always said that racing Cinzano was more like being a grateful passenger than a rider, only needing to count how many times we had to go around. I barely felt him jumping, it was like he simply stretched in the air. Never had to tell him a single thing (believe me, he didn't want to hear it anyway). Just steer the rocket and glory in the

ride. Wow, indeed.

We galloped our 'chasers at a nearby training track to get them fit. And yikes was Cinzano ever a tough gallop. He ran off with all of us exercise riders multiple times. Pull your arms right out of their sockets it seemed. Felt like a power boat at speed. He lived to go fast.

Yet back at the barn he was so chill, my tiny nieces could ride him bareback around the shed row. The Michael Jordan of horses.

For the reasons already mentioned, this was the only race he was able to run that season. Yet another year passed without rivals or competition, spent entirely enjoying farm life, fox hunts, and strolls through the meadows. As I mentioned a few pages earlier, one of Cinzano's tasks was herding cattle, but bovines were also his kryptonite. Not only was the right knot a source of fear for the horse, but he was also terrified of cows. The reason? Shortly after arriving at the estate, Randy Rouse was herding cattle while riding the son of Tudor Park when a cow charged at the horse and rammed him. That incident left a lasting impression on him for the rest of his life, as Michele aptly points out:

Although, to his dying day, Cinzano was deathly afraid of COWS. And we have tons of herds of cows in our country in Virginia. More than once Sir Cinzano planted my sorry butt on the ground when he shied at them. But as I said, he was a true gentleman and always waited for me to get back up and get back on. Too funny.

The 1987 season was the final chapter of Cinzano's sporting career, and he competed entirely in the female jockeys' category under the ride of Michele O'Brien Rouse. As Michele herself would later admit, the horse was not in good health, as the injury to his knot had worsened over the years. However, she didn't realize the severity of it at the time and relied on her husband's expertise. Looking back, she regretted that Randy made him race that year, stating that "it gave Cinzano a farewell he didn't deserve." But let's not get ahead of ourselves.

Although it was the least successful year of his career (one victory, two second places, and a third in five races), the debut at the Casanova meet was as usual: a victory by twenty-five lengths and a double win in the Spring Roads. They didn't know it at the time, but this would be the last victory for the partnership between Michele and Cinzano.

Six days later, they competed in Mt. Salem over 3200 meters, and that March 7 will go down in history for the protagonists as the day Splashy Lea and Patti Cassel took their revenge on Cinzano, who suffered his third defeat in seven years. The race time was 3 minutes 55 seconds 1/5, nearly twenty seconds faster than the other race held in the female jockeys' category, which shows that despite the pain, his rivals had to push themselves to the limit to beat him.

A fourteen-day break and back to the races, because one cannot miss the Warrenton meet. Unfortunately, here the horse finished third, behind Lyle's Turn and Baron Zantippy, two racers who, under normal circumstances, were far from Cinzano's level. But that mattered little in the three miles of the Warrenton Hunt Cup. A week later, the duo would finish second in Piedmont, and on April 11 at Old Dominion, the least desired outcome for our hero would unfold.

> By the time Cinz and I fell in 1987, he was past his prime. I know now that he had lameness issues of which I was unaware at the time. I'm sorry that Randy chose to keep running him. The fall was NOT Cinzano's fault. We were going a blisteringly fast pace with the other front runner. When we got to the next jump, Cinzy's blood was up. He had the heart of a lion. He left the ground a full two strides before the jump. When he was younger and sounder he did that easily so many times. But this time, his hindlegs gave way on take-off. He hit the fence really hard and flipped in the air. He was hurt. I was hurt...broke my leg and ankle...but it was nothing compared to my broken heart. I had hurt The Great One. We both recovered with time, but that was our last race.

William McCormick had already mentioned it in his account: due to his speed, it was common for Cinzano to leave one or two strides between the start of the jump and the hurdle, but this time his health failed him, and in the record of his final race, the letter "F" for Fall appears. It's not a stain on his career, but it is, at the very least, an injustice.

After his retirement from the tracks, he continued to lead the fox hunts and accompanied the couple on countless horseback rides. The flashes faded, and although he occasionally appeared in the "Society" section of Virginia newspapers as an attraction at some dinner or lunch organized by the Rouse family, his retirement was a joy spent in the open fields.

> The races he ran in with us were not money, only huge amounts of prestige. Steeplechase Racing in this part of Virginia is enormously popular, and races are hotly contested. The crowd at the races always cheered Cinzy. He had a huge fan club, especially because of his story. Lots of people have told me that they came to the races mostly just to see Cinzano run. Cinzano was so famous in Virginia. People still talk about him. Early in my own racing career I was lucky enough to ride him in a few races. I've sat on literally thousands of horses since, but none have ever matched the dream rides Cinzy gave me. He was a true gentleman always. A sweet delight around the barn. After Cinz retired from racing, both Randy and I foxhunted him for years. Of course he was perfect at that as well.

It was Michele again who spoke; if I keep quoting her letters, I'll have to list her as a co-author of the book. Cinzano lived with the Rouse-O'Brien family until 1999, when, at the age of twenty-six, his enormous heart finally gave out. I have the theory (impossible to prove) that his longevity was intentional: he wanted to return to his owners the years they had given him when no one else believed in him. In 2007, Cinzano and Randy were inducted into the Virginia Steeplechase Association Hall of Fame, during the annual spring celebration in Middleburg to present the awards for each season. Michele clarifies that not every year does someone get inducted into the Hall of Fame, only when the chosen horse or person is a legend. "Cinzy was such a cool dude, he would've walked right in and headed straight for the buffet table! They all gave Cinzy a standing ovation when it was announced."

Cinzano's remains were laid to rest at Randy Rouse's estate alongside other historic horses, but unfortunately, after Randy's death in 2017, the trust sold the property and turned the former farm into a residential area, thus destroying one of Virginia's historical landmarks. This is a fact that Michele has still not been able to overcome:

> After Randy passed, his Trustees sold our farm where we buried Cinzano. I live on a much smaller farm about 15 miles away now. Our old farm was sold to developers who've built tons of houses there. I'm sure there

aren't any markers left where we buried all our champions. I had no say in the matter and remain sick over it. But I carry the spirit of every single one in my heart every single day. A special place for Cinzy. He was our Secretariat.

"He was our Secretariat" could serve as the last line of this book, but since I didn't write it, I hesitate to close here. It might, however, make the perfect closing line for the movie—stay tuned for that.

Beyond the movie-worthy life Cinzano lived, I'd like to close by highlighting the numbers from his racing career to truly illustrate the exceptional horse he was. It wasn't just his aura that set him apart—he proved his greatness time and again, whether in Brazil, the United States, or at home in Uruguay.

- Uruguay: 8 races ran, 7 wins (including the Polla de Potrillos or Colt Derby , National G. P., G. P. José Pedro Ramírez y Municipal G. P.), 1 second place (at the Jockey Club G. P.).

- Brazil: 1 race ran, 1 fifth place at the São Paulo G. P. with all of the setbacks detailed.

- USA, racetracks: 3 races ran, 1 win.

- USA, fences, timber: 27 races ran, 19 wins (with a streak of 19 wins and 2 defeats in 7 years).

From the year 2007, he was inducted into the Virginia Steeplechase Association Hall of Fame.

- USA, flat, amateur: 3 races ran, 3 wins.

Cinzano's total of thirty wins out of forty-two races strongly supports the concept of "the best horse I've ever ridden" held by all the jockeys who had the privilege of riding him in the Virginia Circuit. This impressive record is a testament to his ability and talent, though, but in the world of horse racing, discussions and the "what if…" will always remain open. Was he really that good? Was he better than Mogambo, his only defeat in South America? Would he have achieved more victories in the U.S. had he not been an "illegal" horse? And were his rivals in Virginia really at his level? While these questions are valid, the world of racing offers no absolute certainties—only opinions and memories shaped by those who witnessed the Cinzano phenomenon. Though I never saw him race in person, I choose to trust the accounts of those who were close to him and affirm that he was a champion, a convict, and is a legend.

THE AUTHOR

Daniel Torres Rodríguez is a father, husband, architect, and thanks to this book, he is also a writer, or close enough. Born in the city of Colonia del Sacramento, Uruguay, in 1979, since his childhood, he has been passionate about horse racing and reading (in that order). Since 2006, he has been part of the staff at En Una Baldosa, a famous Argentine sports website, and since 2010, he has been collaborating with the digital magazine Eleturf. This is his first book, and who knows if it won"t be his last.

INDEX

Made in the USA
Columbia, SC
23 May 2025